# *RENEW*

# ORIENTATION BOOKLET

The contents of this study are in accordance with the Statements of Faith of the National Association of Evangelicals (USA) and the Evangelical Fellowship of India.

The following abbreviations refer to the following reference works. The commentary series represent various titles and dates of which the authors will be noted in the study:

BDAG  *A Greek-English Lexicon of the New Testament and Early Christian Literature*, F. W. Danker ed., 3rd edition, (University of Chicago).

BENTC  *Baker Exegetical New Testament Commentary* (Baker).

BST  *Bible Speaks Today* (Intervarsity).

EBC  *Expositors Bible Commentary* (Zondervan).

NICNT  *New International Commentary on the New Testament* (Eerdmans).

NICOT  *New International Commentary on the Old Testament* (Eerdmans).

NIDNTT  *New International Dictionary of New Testament Theology* (Zondervan).

NIGTC  *New International Greek Testament Commentary* (Eerdmans).

PNTC  *Pillar New Testament Commentary* (Eerdmans).

TNTC  *Tyndale New Testament Commentary* (Eerdmans).

TWOT  *Theological Wordbook of the Old Testament* (Moody).

Vine's  *Vine's Complete Expository Dictionary of Old and New Testament Words*, W. E. Vine (Thomas Nelson).

WBC  *Word Biblical Commentary* (Word).

*Webster's  Merriam-Webster Dictionary*; online at www.merriam-webster.com.

# RENEW
## *Orientation Booklet*

## Chapters

**Chapter 1**:  God's Promise to Change Your Life   p. 1

**Chapter 2:** Renew Ministry: A Powerful Tool to Transform Your Life
p. 8

**Chapter 3**:  Helpful Hints to Experience an Effective Renew Ministry
Session   p. 15
Project 1: Review the Primary Principles of Renew Ministry

**Chapter 4**:  The Seven Steps in a Renew Ministry Session   p. 27
Project 2: Review the Renew Ministry Steps

**Chapter 5**:  Renew Ministry Requirement I: Humility   p. 44

**Chapter 6**:  Renew Ministry Requirement II: Hard Work    p. 53

**Chapter 7**:  Renew Ministry Requirement III: A Heart for God   p. 63

Chapter 1
# God's Promise to Change Your Life
Romans 12:2

A middle-aged Christian woman testifies:

If someone could travel back in time and see me a few years ago they would not recognize me now. I devoted the first ten years of my Christian life to Bible study and prayer. But the effect of Renew Ministry on my life has been to completely renew my mind in a way that was previously impossible. I have found freedom from habitual sins, allowing me to grow into a deeper relationship with God.

Is it possible to radically and permanently change your life? Yes! Did God intend for you to constantly struggle with controlling negative emotions like anger, anxiety, and discouragement? No! Why are we so confident about these things? Because like the Christian woman above, we have witnessed many people who have overcome these things through a process called Renew Ministry. It is a ministry based on biblical principles and a proven process to help God's people experience His promise to:

**Be transformed by the renewing of your mind.** (Romans 12:2 NIV)

God promises that you will change your life when you change your mind.

## A) God's promise to transform your life [1]

Romans 12:2 is one of the most powerful promises in all of God's word. The original Greek word used for "*transformed*" is *metamorphos*. It means a RADICAL and PERMANENT CHANGE in the character or appearance of something or someone. [2] The Apostle could not have chosen a stronger Greek word to communicate being "*transformed*."

The biblical idea of transformation means RADICAL change. As NT scholar John Stott notes, Romans 12:2 is describing "a fundamental transformation of character and conduct, away from the standards of the world and into the image of Christ himself." [3] God is promising YOU CAN

CHANGE ANYTHING ABOUT YOUR CHARACTER in a revolutionary and lasting way. There is nothing about your moral weaknesses that cannot be changed, no matter how long you have been that way, or how hard you have tried to change it. God wants to help you change it because He loves you and He wants to be glorified through your life.

Why does mind renewal create such a RADICAL transformation of our character? Because when you renew your mind you will be trusting more truth and trusting the truth empowers the Holy Spirit to more consistently control you.

Secondly, God is promising PERMANENT change. When you are "*transformed*" the new you is the natural and consistent way you will live. When you are "*transformed by the renewing of your mind*" you will no longer have to force yourself to be different. You will simply and naturally be different. Being "*transformed by the renewing of your mind*" will require hard work. But AFTER you have been "*transformed*" you no longer need to work to maintain your transformation. It is PERMANENT. That is what transformation (*metamorphos*) means. Far too many Christians are focused on trying to conform their lives to the truth. Instead, they should focus on being transformed by the truth.

Why is mind renewal permanent? Because the Bible says, "*The light shines in the darkness, and the darkness can never extinguish it*" (John 1:5). 4 You cannot bring darkness into a place of light. But you can bring light into a dark place. And once a room has light, darkness cannot invade it. Likewise, lies and truth cannot occupy the same space.

A good illustration of *metamorphos* is the transformation that occurs when a caterpillar turns into a butterfly. First, the change is RADICAL. A caterpillar is ugly and crawls on many legs. The butterfly is beautiful and flies with two wings. Secondly, the change is PERMANENT. A butterfly does not need to keep trying to remain a butterfly. They have been permanently transformed into something else. A butterfly naturally flies because that is what they have been changed into. And notice that a butterfly cannot turn back into a caterpillar. Once changed, always changed. And this is true of the spiritual growth and transformation that the Bible is talking about.

God promises that you will change your life when you change your mind. This is because you will: "*Be transformed by the renewing of your mind*" (Rom 12:2).

## B) God's command to renew your mind

Again, Romans 12:2 is one of the most powerful promises in God's word. But it is not an unconditional promise that God will fulfill regardless of what you do. Romans 12:2 is not only a promise, but includes a command: "Renew your mind." God promises you will be transformed if you renew your mind. This answers an important question asked by many Christians: What is God's part and my part in spiritual growth? God has already done His part by giving you the truth that can set you free from the power of sin (cf. John 8:31-36). Your part is to use that truth to renew your mind and be transformed.

Many Christians are confused about the most important questions in the Christian life: How do you grow spiritually? How do you become more like Christ? How do you become a more loving, joyful, peaceful, and fruitful Christian? The biblical answer is the promise and command of Romans 12:2: "*Be transformed by the renewing of your mind.*" There is always and only one way that you spiritually grow in a lasting way: renew your mind.

Many Christians put a great deal of effort into changing their circumstances because they believe it will make them happier. Think of all the time, effort, and peace lost in changing jobs, churches, friendships, and possessions. And then we quickly discover we are no happier. How do we truly experience more happiness? Pursuing God's command to change our mind instead of our circumstances. And when we do, we will be surprised how many circumstances we can be happy in!

What does the command to renew your mind mean? Renewing your mind is replacing the LIES you believe about yourself, with God's TRUTH. The Apostle Paul describes those who have a depraved mind as those who have "*exchanged the truth about God for a lie*" (Rom. 1:25 NIV). The Christian seeks to do the opposite: to exchange the lies we believe for the Lord's truth, leading to a renewed mind and a transformed life. Mind renewal is not adding more biblical knowledge on top of the lies we believe. Rather, it is replacing lies we believe with the Lord's truth.

The only way any Christian experiences radical and permanent change is to replace the lies that control them with the truth that grows them. You can do all kinds of Christian activities including praying, fasting, and Bible study, or you can go through difficult challenges. But if these activities or experiences do not change your mind, they will not change your life.

Why do you change your life when you change your mind? Because your mind is the control center of your life. It is where you believe, and everything you do is controlled by what you truly believe. The Bible says of all humans: *"For as he thinks within himself, so he is"* (Prov 23:7 NASB [5]). This is why the Bible says, *"Above all else, guard your heart, for everything you do flows from it"* (Prov 4:23 NIV). Your beliefs determine what you will do and who you will be. This is how God created you.

If you change what you believe, you will change what you desire and feel. And because you act on what you desire and feel, all of this will change your character. And because you can permanently change your beliefs, you can permanently change your character. This is not pagan psychology. This is biblical doctrine.

There is another reason that mind renewal uniquely transforms the Christian. As explained elsewhere in the *Christian Essentials Faith Study*:

> TRUSTING the TRUTH turns on the power of the Holy Spirit in your life. TRUSTING LIES turns on the power of the sinful nature. It is that simple. Every time you sin it is because you are believing a LIE. Every time you experience the love, joy, peace, power, and holiness of the Holy Spirit, it is because at that moment you are TRUSTING the TRUTH. This is one of the most vital things to understand about the Christian life. [6]

The permanently and radically transformed Christian life is empowered by being consistently controlled by God's Spirit in you. And renewing your mind is the only way for that to happen.

Do you see the biblical pattern and plan for spiritual growth and life transformation? Note this carefully because this answers those important questions that many Christians do not understand: How do you grow spiritually? How do you become more like Christ? How do you become a more loving, joyful, peaceful, and fruitful Christian? The biblical answer is explained in the following four steps:

1) Because you love God, make it your goal to obey Him and *"<u>Imitate God</u> in everything you do"* (Eph 5:1). Do not set your sights lower

than that, because becoming like Him is His expectation for your life.

2) Let the current level of love you have for God motivate you to pursue obeying Romans 12:2. This may be the hardest thing you do in the Christian life, but your love for God will empower you to do it.

3) Be transformed by renewing the logical and subconscious parts of your mind so you will trust the truth of God's love in more places of your heart and life.

4) Then you will be more consistently controlled by God the Spirit who lives inside of you, and will effortlessly and automatically experience His power to obey God so that His commandments are that "*easy*" and "*light*" yoke that Jesus promised (cf. Matt 11:28-30).

Notice that obeying Romans 12:2 is the starting point for all of the above. Therefore, we would argue that the commandment that requires the most painful work and perseverance to actually obey may be to "*be transformed by the renewing of your mind*" (Rom 12:2). We would also argue that Romans 12:2 is among the most important command in the Bible to obey.

This is because <u>after</u> you obey the command to "*be transformed by the renewing of your mind*," you will automatically, effortlessly, and joyfully obey all the rest of God's commands. If you do the painful and hard work of "*renewing your mind*" you will "*be transformed*" into a person consistently controlled by the Holy Spirit so that all the rest of God's commands become the easy yoke and the light burden that Christ promised (cf. Matt 11:30). In fact, it is only by being "*transformed by the renewing of your mind*" that you <u>can</u> actually obey <u>any</u> of God's commands in a God-pleasing way, no matter how hard you try to do otherwise.

How consistently and completely will you obey the Greatest Commandment to "*love the LORD your God with all your heart, all your soul, all your mind, and all your strength*" (Mark 12:30)? It completely depends on how diligently and completely you obey the command to "*be transformed by the renewing of your mind*" (Rom 12:2). All of this is why we suggest that Romans 12:2 is among the hardest and the most important of all God's commands to obey.

Therefore, we see this necessary "upward spiral" of synergy between renewing our mind and loving God. Which comes first? Renewing our mind. Our initial conversion to Christ demonstrated that. We had no real love for God <u>before</u> we were "*transformed by the renewing of your mind*" with the truth of God's love in the Gospel. And now we must apply all the love for God we have obtained through mind renewal, in order to be motivated to pursue more mind renewal, so we will love God even more.

Yes, in Renew Ministry you will learn that renewing those hidden, hurting, and hardened parts of your heart may be the hardest commandment to obey. But the transformation you experience by doing so, will also teach you that Romans 12:2 is among the most important commands to obey. Because when you do, the power of the Holy Spirit will be greater in your life, enabling you to obey all the rest of God's commands automatically and effortlessly.

Do all Christians need mind renewal? Do you need this? Yes! Romans 12:2 is a command to all Christians to "*be transformed by the renewing of your mind.*" The Greek word translated "renewing" (*anakainōsei*) is in the present tense, indicating that "renewing of the mind is a continuing process" [7] for all Christians.

Everyone believes lies, and because of this, everyone needs to have their minds renewed. Coming out of our denial of our true spiritual state is the first step toward spiritual growth. If you doubt you need transformation, then complete *the FRUIT Study.* [8] It reminds you that God lives in you and should be living through you so that you consistently experience His love, joy, and peace (being spiritually FREER! and FRUITFUL). It is consistent anger, anxiety, lust, shame, and depression that indicate we need more mind renewal.

Which is why God promises that you will change your life when you change your mind. This is because you will: "*Be transformed by the renewing of your mind*" (Rom 12:2).

---

[1] Sections A and B here are essentially repeated in chapter 2.3 of *Christian Essentials* study #2, *FOUNDATIONS*. However, these biblical truths are so important, they are worth repeating in the *FREEDOM* study as well.

[2] *BDAG* defines *metamorphos* as: "to change inwardly in fundamental character or condition, be changed, be transformed."

3 John Stott, *The Message of Romans* (Intervarsity, 1994), 323.

4 The NIV translates John 1:5 as *"The light shines in the darkness, and the darkness has not overcome it."* The word *"overcome"* translates the Greek word *katelaben*. Leon Morris writes: "It contains the idea of laying hold of something so as to make it one's own (cf. its translations as "gets" with reference to a prize, 1 Cor. 9:24)" (*The Gospel According to John* [Eerdmans, 1995], 76).

This general meaning leads to some versions taking it to mean "lay hold of with the mind" and thus *"comprehend"* (KJV, NKJV, NASB). But most translations render it as *"overcome"* (NIV, ESV, HCSB, NCV). Morris adds, "We do not usually talk of darkness as trying to 'understand' light. . .   The verb has a rarer but sufficiently attested meaning, "overcome'. It is that that is required here" (Ibid.). Likewise, D. A. Carson adds, "In the only other passage in the Fourth Gospel where the verb is used with the light/darkness metaphor, the meaning 'to overcome' is required by the context (John 12:35)" (*The Gospel According to John* [Eerdmans, 1991], 138).

5 (Prov 23:7)- The NASB gives the literal translation of the Hebrew. While most translations note this as an alternative meaning in their margin, they abandon the literal meaning of the Hebrew in an effort to better reflect the context of a warning not to eat food offered by a stingy person (cf. v. 6). So, the NIV has, *"for he is the kind of person who is always thinking about the cost."* But the words "the cost" are not in the Hebrew text.

Nevertheless, the more literal translation fits the context well. If a person thinks in stingy ways, they will be stingy. The TEV captures this well, translating v. 7 *"'Come on and have some more,' he says, but he doesn't mean it. What he thinks is what he really is."*

Thus *K&D* translate with "most moderns . . . 'as he reckons in his soul, so is he.'" Likewise, OT scholar Bruce Waltke translates the verse: "as he calculates within himself, so is he" and comments, "his inner thinking exposes his true identity" (*The Book of Proverbs*, Vol. 2, *NICOT* [Eerdmans, 2005], 227, 242). Thus, a good translation would be: *"What he thinks in his heart, he will be in his life."* The more literal translation preserves a valuable biblical statement on the psychology of humanity.

6 For more on the relationship between trusting truth and being controlled by God's Spirit see the section on the Spirit's Power in *Christian Essentials* study #3: *FAITH*.

7 Douglas Moo, *The Epistle to the Romans* (Eerdmans, 1996), 756.

8 The *FRUIT* study is an important introduction to this booklet as well as the Freedom Study. If you have not completed them, you are encouraged to do so.

Chapter 2
# Renew Ministry: A Powerful Tool to Transform Your Life
Romans 12:2

---

**Be transformed by the renewing of your mind.** (Rom 12:2 NIV)

Renew Ministry is a proven process based on biblical principles that will change your life.

## A) The proven power of Renew Ministry: Experiencing the Spirit more consistently

This study is an introduction to Renew Ministry. Renew Ministry is a proven process for obeying God's command to renew your mind and experience transformation (cf. Rom 12:2). It is not something new. The Bible speaks repeatedly about the power of changing your life by changing your mind (Ps 42:5; 9 Prov 4:23; 23:7; John 8:31-36; Rom 12:2; 2 Cor 10:3-5; Eph 3:18-19; 6:16; Phil 1:9; 4:8; Col 1:10; 3:10; 1 Pet 2:1-2). We have simply put the process of mind renewal into an intentional system, and targeted the subconscious/emotional part of the mind where most of our controlling lies exist.

Radical and permanent change in character has been a proven effect of Renew Ministry. We have all heard many claims about something that will change your life. But the proposed program or product does not work as advertised. This is not true of the biblical principles and proven process in Renew Ministry. The numerous testimonies throughout the FREEDOM Study, FRUIT Study and the Renew Ministry Training Manual, will demonstrate this.

Renew Ministry may be the most significant spiritual journey you will ever experience. This is what many would claim who have applied it to their lives. This is because being radically and permanently *"transformed by the renewing of your mind"* (Rom 12:2) is a powerful experience with life-changing and lasting effects on every area of your life, including your love, joy, peace, marriage, parenting, work, and ministry.

We noted in the previous chapter that biblical transformation means a permanent change. That is what people experience in Renew Ministry.

People often ask after a session, "What do I need to do to make sure the lie I believed doesn't return?" The answer is: "Nothing!" The power of biblical transformation and Renew Ministry is permanent. There may be other parts of your mind that are imprinted with a lie, but the part that is renewed will remain convinced of the truth.

We asked in the previous chapter, why does mind renewal create such a RADICAL transformation of our character? Because when you renew your mind you will be trusting more truth. And trusting the truth empowers the Holy Spirit to control you more consistently. And when the Spirit controls you, you have the power to consistently obey the supernatural commands of God and live the authentic Christian life. Remember, *"The kingdom of God is not a matter of talk but of power"* (1 Cor 4:20 NIV).

Unfortunately, modern Christianity makes the common mistake of telling Christians what they are supposed to do, but not helping them have the power to do it! This is what the Pharisees did. And Jesus did not like it. Jesus said:

> *You experts in the law, woe to you, because you load people down with burdens they can hardly carry, and you yourselves will not lift one finger to help them.* (Luke 11:46)

Church leaders do the same when they teach God's people to pursue the commands of Christ, but do not help them experience the power of the Spirit. Many Christians and Christian leaders seem to believe that being <u>indwelled</u> by the Holy Spirit automatically means you will be <u>controlled</u> by the Holy Spirit. No so! Many churches call their people to evangelism projects and discipleship programs and ministry needs. But never ask the question if the people are controlled consistently enough by the POWER of Holy Spirit to actually do these things in a God pleasing way. Much of modern Christian ministry is like giving you detailed instructions on how to operate a computer. But you don't have any electricity!

Likewise, Christian counselors will often listen to your struggle, [10] but then simply tell you what you are supposed TO DO. Which you probably already knew anyway. Most Christian discipleship materials and programs merely do the same. Teaching people biblical commands but not teaching them how to consistently experience the supernatural power necessary to obey them is another form of exhausting legalism.

As a result, many Christians are living what we described in the previous *FRUIT* study as COPING Christianity: trying to live the Christian life in your own human will power instead of the Spirit's power. The common lack of unconditional and supernatural love, joy, peace, patience, self-control, and POWER in Christian lives and churches is proving that. So is the high numbers of Christians and Christian leaders who are experiencing spiritual "burn out."

Renew Ministry *"is not a matter of talk but of power"* (1 Cor 4:20). We are not interested in simply helping you to cope better. Rather, we are serious about enabling people to consistently experience the power of God living in them and through them. This is the FREER! Christianity also described in the previous *Christian Essentials* study *FRUIT*. [11]

Remember what God promises and commands. Be radically and permanently *"transformed by the renewing of your mind"* (Rom 12:2)! How can this actually happen? Renew Ministry is a proven process based on biblical principles that will change your life.

## B) The revolutionary target of Renew Ministry: Your hidden heart

We have received many testimonies from people who say that Renew Ministry has been much more effective than traditional Christian or secular counseling. Why is this? Because it has a different target than typical counseling. We believe that when the Bible says, *"Be transformed by the renewing of your mind"* (Rom 12:2), it must include the hidden and subconscious parts of your mind. Typical counseling ignores this and only ministers to the conscious/logical mind.

You are not usually aware of what is in your subconscious mind. That is why it is "sub" or "un" conscious. But the hidden parts of your mind control your life in powerful ways.

For example, do you believe God loves you? Of course, you do. You could not even be a Christian if you did not believe God loves you. You know God demonstrated His love for you by having His Son die for your sins on a cross (cf. Rom 5:8). You believe the Bible verses you have memorized about God's love. If someone claimed that God does not love

His children, we would immediately, automatically, and confidently conclude they were foolish and deceived.

Then why do you still struggle with worry, selfishness, lust, and discouragement? Why are you so hurt and offended when people do not love you? If you <u>really</u> and completely believed in God's love for you, then you would not care what people think of you and you would be free from all of these things.

Why can't you consistently live what you believe? <u>Because you do not believe it with your whole mind</u>. Your logical conscious mind probably believes in God's love as much as is humanly possible. But there are parts of your irrational subconscious mind that do not believe in God's love. Therefore, when those parts of your mind get "triggered," you feel and act anger, worry, and other sins as if God does not love you.

Therefore, the key to "*Be transformed by the renewing of your mind*" is getting the power of God's truth to the hidden, hurting, deceived, and controlling parts of your subconscious mind. Ignoring this truth is why so much Christian ministry, teaching, disciplines, and counseling is ineffective to change our lives radically and permanently. It is wrongly but widely believed that Christians simply need to understand or memorize <u>more</u> biblical truth to be changed. But the fact is this: MOST CHRISTIANS ALREADY KNOW THE TRUTH THEY NEED. IT JUST NEEDS TO BE EXPERIENCED IN MORE PLACES OF THEIR MIND.

This is why you will fail to "*demolish strongholds*" (2 Cor 10:3 NIV) of controlling lies if you only add more knowledge to your conscious/logical mind and ignore renewing the subconscious/emotional parts of your mind. Unfortunately, a typical counseling session looks something like this. You tell the counselor your problems and they give you some answers. The assumption is that you did not know these things before, or that you need to be more convinced of them.

But usually you already know the truth a counselor is telling you. The problem is not faulty logic or knowledge as many counselors assume. The problem is that there are hidden parts of your mind that have not experienced the truth your logical conscious mind already knows to be true. But because typical counseling primarily targets the logical conscious mind, it does not renew the part of your mind that actually needs it. It is because Renew Ministry is uniquely designed to effectively heal the hidden and hurting parts of your heart, that it has a unique ability to change your life radically and permanently.

Unfortunately, many Christians doubt the influence of their subconscious mind. They think such a concept has only come from secular psychology. However, in chapters 14-16 of the FREEDOM Study we demonstrate that the Bible speaks clearly about the hidden parts of our mind and our need to minister to them.

So how do you get those truths from your "head" to your "heart"? The biblical principles and proven process of Renew Ministry enables you to do that and believe God's freeing and empowering truth with your "whole heart."

God promises and commands *"be transformed by the renewing of your mind"* (Rom 12:2)! How can this actually happen? Renew Ministry is a proven process based on biblical principles that will change your life.

## C) The radically different method of Renew Ministry: Asking questions instead of giving truth

Some might call Renew Ministry counseling. But it is radically different in method than typical counseling. Renew Ministry does not require that someone knows all the ANSWERS to your problems. In fact, it does not require them to know any ANSWERS, or a huge store of theological knowledge, or life experience to help you.

This is because Renew Ministry is essentially a set of prescribed QUESTIONS that enable a person to reveal and renew the hidden and hurting parts of their heart. Proverbs says, *"The purposes of a person's heart are deep waters, but one who has insight draws them out"* (20:5 NIV). There is no better way to "draw out" the deep things of a person's heart than the skillful use of questions.

Because Renew Ministry is ministering to your subconscious mind, you might assume the process is complicated. But it is relatively simple. The same questions have been proven over many years to help people renew the hidden and hurting parts of their mind. Virtually any caring person can learn how to effectively use the Renew Ministry QUESTIONS. In fact, many have even learned to use Renew Ministry on themselves and practice it regularly.

Therefore, Renew Ministry does not require lengthy training or the expertise of a Pastor or professional counselor. Because of its simplicity, Renew Ministry enables a local church to actually obey the often-ignored NT command to effectively *"counsel each other"* (Col 3:16). Obeying this command is vital to the Church today.

The need for effective mind renewal among Christians, and the personal attention it requires, is far too great for Renew Ministry to be confined and limited to Pastors and professionals. And the Renew Ministry process is simple enough for this to happen. In fact, we have often heard others say it has been more helpful to them than professional counseling. The simplicity of Renew Ministry is the reason we are so confident that virtually any trusted Christian friend or spouse can effectively help you through the Renew Ministry process.

Renew Ministry is really NOT counseling, therapy, Bible teaching, or spiritual guidance. Nor is the relationship between Renew Ministry Helpers and Recipients like a counselor/counselee or doctor/patient relationship. In fact, we strongly encourage all Christians to be both Recipients and Helpers in Renew Ministry and to obey Colossians 3:16 to *"counsel each other."*

We do not claim that Renew Ministry is the <u>only</u> effective tool for renewing the mind. But after many years of research and experience, Renew Ministry has proven to be a very effective tool to help Christians experience real, lasting spiritual transformation through mind renewal.

God promises and commands *"be transformed by the renewing of your mind"* (Rom 12:2)! How can this actually happen? Renew Ministry is a proven process based on biblical principles that will change your life.

## D) The challenges of Renew Ministry

Renew Ministry is biblical, powerful, and simple. But it is not easy. We want to be honest with you about that. As noted above, many people have testified that Renew Ministry and the spiritual freedom it brings has been the most important and wonderful spiritual journey of their life. They experienced God in ways they never have before. But they would also testify that Renew Ministry was the hardest thing they have ever done.

Why is being *"transformed by the renewing of your mind"* (Rom 12:2) so difficult? First, most Christians have been imprinted with more controlling lies in their hidden mind than they could ever imagine. They need more mind renewal than they think.

Secondly, healing those hidden and hurting parts of your mind will require facing the painful emotions that are there. Renew Ministry helps you experience the love, truth, power, and light of Jesus in those hurting, deceived, stubborn, and dark places within you. But there is no way to reveal the lies that control you unless you face the pain those lies are causing. Yes, being *"transformed by the renewing of our mind"* will bring a lot more love, joy, peace, and control into your life. But the challenges on the journey will teach you some very valuable things as well.

God promises and commands *"be transformed by the renewing of your mind"* (Rom 12:2)! How can this actually happen? Renew Ministry is a proven process based on biblical principles that will change your life.

▶ If you have not gone through the previous *FRUIT or FREEDOM Study*, you should do so as soon as possible. It will give you more important biblical principles about mind renewal and additional motivation to pursue spiritual healing.

---

[9] For an explanation of the powerful mind renewal being described in Psalm 42, see the *FRUIT* study, chapters 7-9.

[10] Many approaches to counseling reflect a belief that simply talking about the problem will solve it. Along these lines, trauma expert Dr. Bessel van der Kolk writes regarding a study of Post Traumatic Stress Disorder:

> Perhaps the most important finding in our study was that remembering the trauma with all its associated affects, does not necessarily resolve it. Most of our study participants could tell a coherent story and also experience the pain associated with those stories, but they kept being haunted by unbearable images and physical sensations. Research in contemporary exposure treatment, a staple of cognitive behavioral therapy, has similarly disappointing results: The majority of patients treated with that method continue to have serious PTSD symptoms three months after the end of treatment. . .

> Traditional psychotherapy has focused mainly on constructing a narrative that explains why a person feels a particular way . . . Telling the story is important . . . But, telling a story about the event does not guarantee that the traumatic memories will be laid to rest. (*The Body Keeps the Score* (Penguin, 2014, Kindle ed.), 194, 219.

[11] For more on the levels of spiritual health, including COPING and FREER! Christianity, see section III of the *FRUIT Study*.

# Chapter 3

# Helpful Hints to Experience an Effective Renew Ministry Session

## A) What is a Renew Ministry Session?

Essentially, a Renew Ministry session is a 1-2 hour meeting with a Renew Ministry Helper. As a Renew Ministry Recipient you will basically be asked a prescribed set of questions. They are designed to get you in touch with your negative and painful feelings so you can locate deceived and hurting parts of your heart, discover the Identity Lie causing those feelings, and experience the truth of God's love to renew your mind.

The primary purpose of a Renew Ministry session is not to give you advice or tell you the truth. Again, most Christians do not need any more truth. What they need is to get the truth they already have, to the places in their heart that do not have it. This is best accomplished by simply being asked questions. Therefore, the best Renew Ministry Helpers will spend the entire session only asking you questions.

There are seven steps in a Renew Ministry session:

1) CONNECT

2) FEELING

3) EXPERIENCE

4) LIE

5) JESUS

6) TRUTH

7) REVIEW

Each Step has a specific purpose that is accomplished by answering the prescribed questions. In the next chapter we will discuss these steps in more detail. In this chapter we will explain what you, as the Recipient, can do to make your sessions most effective.

## B) The <u>two most important things</u> for a Renew Ministry Recipient to do during a session

### 1) Answer the questions with <u>the very first thing</u> that comes to mind.

Remember, the target of the questions in a Renew Ministry session is your emotional, irrational, subconscious mind. Therefore, the answers we are looking for will be emotional and irrational. We are wanting to discover the lies that hidden parts of your heart believe, so we need to let them "speak." We are not looking for the logically "correct" answers, but the answer that a hurting and deceived part of you believes. Again, this is because we are wanting to work with your "heart" not your "head."

You may think in response to a question: "I know that is not true or right, but that is how I feel." Yes, and you need to express the answer that this deceived part of you feels. This indicates you are working with your emotional and irrational subconscious mind. Just answer the questions with the first thing that comes to mind, no matter how illogical or even sinful it might be. Again, we have to let these deceived and even sinful parts of you "speak" in order to know what they believe.

When you are struggling to answer the Renew Ministry questions with the first thing that comes to mind, this usually indicates a Guarding Part is operating. These Guarding Parts do not want the deceived and sinful parts of your heart exposed and therefore will try to have you stay in your logical mind. What will that look like?

- You want to "analyze" your answer to a question to make sure it is the "correct" one before speaking it.
- You try to "figure out" your problem.
- You monitor the process, or keep track of where you are in the session.
- You try to anticipate the Helper's questions.

These kinds of thoughts usually indicate a Guarding Part that will interfere with the session.

So, the most important thing for a Renew Ministry Recipient to do in a session is to answer the questions with the first thing that comes to their mind.

## 2) Report <u>any</u> hesitancy, resistance, or distractions in responding to the questions.

If there is anything happening in your thoughts other than focusing on answering the Helper's questions, then report this to your Helper so they can help you resolve it and make progress in the session. Common examples include: going blank, having no emotion, being distracted with other thoughts, feeling embarrassed, etc. If you sense any interference, hesitancy, resistance, or distraction from answering a question in the session, simply report this to your Helper.

Any mental interference to answering a question usually indicates a Guarding Part. These are the most common cause of an ineffective Renew Ministry session. Therefore, your Helper needs your assistance to recognize them if they occur during a session. Do not try to "push through" a session or simply ignore interference. It is important to recognize and resolve any Guarding Parts along the way to a successful Renew Ministry session.

Finally, before you come to a session, think about how you feel about the session. Do you sense any hesitancy or bad emotions about going to the session itself? Report these to your Helper at the beginning of your session so they too can be resolved.

The 2 most important things that a Renew Ministry Recipient can do to help ensure an effective session is: 1) Answer the questions with the very first thing that comes to mind; 2) Report <u>any</u> hesitancy, resistance, or distractions in responding to the questions.

## C) Other encouragements for an effective Renew Ministry session

### 1) You cannot fail

You might be concerned that if you do not do all the right things, a session will fail. Or you may be discouraged if you do not complete all 6 Steps of Renew Ministry in one session. But understand God is pleased with whatever efforts you are making to overcome sin in your life. Pleasing God is success in the Christian life. Therefore, if you are simply doing your best to do your part in a session, this pleases God and you cannot fail.

Remember, all that is really expected of you is to do your best to do the two things described above: 1) Answer the questions with the very first thing that comes to mind; 2) Report <u>any</u> hesitancy, resistance, or distractions in responding to the questions. If you simply do your best to do that in a session, your session will please God regardless of its outcome.

However, every step you do complete in a Renew Ministry session is progress in mind renewal, even if you do not complete all the steps in one session. For example, even attempting the first step FEELINGS can be significant progress for many people. They have never talked about their painful emotions before, and doing so is the first step to getting them resolved.

Therefore, be patient with yourself and the process. If mind renewal and freedom from your past, was easy, everybody would experience it more. And remember, you are dealing with the most complex thing in all of Creation: the human mind! Sometimes issues will need to be resolved in layers and will not occur all at once. Just keep persisting in the Renew Ministry Process and mind renewal will occur.

## 2) No pain no gain.

Understand you must feel the pain, in order to heal it. There is no other way to heal the hurting parts of your heart. You must embrace and experience their pain in order to realize the Identity Lie causing the pain and resolve it.

This is why the experience of God's truth and love in these places is so powerful. You are experiencing them in the midst of pain. God wants you to experience His love in a way that *"surpasses knowledge"* (Eph 3:19 NIV). And experiencing it in your emotional/subconscious mind, instead of merely the logical mind is what makes the difference. Dr. van der Kolk writes:

> People cannot put traumatic events behind until they are able to acknowledge what has happened and start to recognize the invisible demons they're struggling with. . . . In order to regain control over your self, you need to revisit the trauma: Sooner or later you need to confront what has happened to you . . . Relief does not come until we are able to acknowledge what has happened and recognize the invisible demons we're struggling with. [12]

## 3) Do not overlook small emotions or events

Many times in the Renew Ministry session a small emotion will turn out to be connected to a powerful Hurting Part. It is easy to overlook small emotions in a session and think they are not worth pursuing. But often they are the "tip of an iceberg" that is underneath and controlling your life. Do not ignore or overlook even a little bit of anger, fear, or shame in a session, but report it.

Likewise, do not dismiss apparently small events that might come to mind, especially in the EXPERIENCE step. You may not think you have experienced a lot of traumatic or painful events in our life. Especially compared to others. This does not matter. Even the smallest event in childhood can hurt you deeply and continue to control your life in powerful ways. Do not overlook or ignore seemingly small event. They too may the "the tip of an iceberg."

## 4) Do not be surprised by how strong some of your emotions are

You may encounter parts of you that really hate God. You may encounter parts that really love sin. It is important to embrace and feel these parts in order to discover the lies they believe and resolve them.

In the *FRUIT* study which is one of the two Renew Ministry Books, different stages of spiritual health were discussed. These included DEFEAT, which is when we are struggling with obvious and controlling sin, COPING which when we are suppressing of sin in our own will power, GROWING which is when we are focusing on replacing controlling lies with empowering truth, and FREER! Christianity which is when we are trusting the truth and experiencing the Spirit. In a very real way, a Renew Ministry session takes you through all of these stages.

First, you must be willing to embrace those parts of you that are experiencing spiritual DEFEAT because they are deceived about God and sin. Secondly, you must confront those Guarding Parts that are simply trying to COPE and suppress things in your own will power because of fear, guilt, and shame. Thirdly, you must do the hard work of GROWING by discovering the controlling lies in your hidden heart and replacing them with freeing truth. Only then will you experience God's Spirit more consistently controlling your life which is FREER! Christianity.

## 5) Open & close the box of your feelings

A Renew Ministry session will typically be a very emotional experience. It is important to be as open about your feelings as possible. Usually those negative feelings are completely resolved. We are not exaggerating to say that over 85% of Recipients leave a session feeling very relieved and happier.

But sometimes not all of the painful emotions that were stirred up in a session get resolved. Therefore, as much as possible, you must "put a lid" back on those emotions at the end of the session. Suppressing negative emotions and the COPING Christianity that results, is not God's ultimate goal for your life. But until you are consistently experiencing FREER! Christianity, this is the best and least destructive thing you can do.

As you start your Renew Ministry journey, you may struggle more with emotions than you did before. Things are getting "stirred up." But this is necessary. It has been the lie that you should not stir things up that has kept you in bondage. But as you continue to make progress, this struggle will significantly diminish.

So, you need to "open the box" of your painful emotions in a Renew Ministry session because it is a safe place to do so. But you need to "close the box" on any unresolved emotions until your next session.

As you make more progress, you may be able to do some Renew Ministry on your own. But be careful. Many Recipients attempt to get their negative emotions resolved on their own and end up just being mentally exhausted. If you can make progress on your own, do so. But if a self-session becomes too difficult, stop, and wait to get help.

Some have found it helpful to keep a journal of their emotions throughout the week. This can help them have a place to "put" their negative feelings until a Renew Ministry session. This can also assist you in knowing what feelings to start with in an Renew Ministry session.

## 6) Move forward in faith, not fear or frustration

We never want you to do something in a Renew Ministry session until you are ready to do it. For example, it may be helpful for you to revisit a very painful, scary, and shameful event in your life. We don't want you to "go there" until you have the faith to do so. It is not necessary or helpful to "push through" your fears. Therefore, when we encounter any resistance or hesitation to a step in the Renew Ministry session, we will back up, and resolve the issue before moving forward.

This is why it is important to recognize and resolve Guarding Parts and God Lies along the way. There may be Guarding Parts that will strongly resist you accessing these hurting, controlling, and deceived parts of you. Other Guarding Parts may want to "force" you to "just get this done," and become impatient with the process. But you need to move forward in the process by FAITH, not FEAR or frustration. Recognizing and resolving Guarding Parts and God Lies along the way will enable you to trust and experience Jesus and His peace throughout the process.

## 7) Probably close your eyes

Most Recipients will find it helpful to close their eyes during the session. Again, this is not a typical counseling session where the focus is a dialogue with the counselor. You need to be focused inward on your feelings, not outward on the counselor or anything else. Therefore, closing your eyes will probably help you have this inward focus.

## 8) Use your imagination if it is helpful to you

People process lies and truth in different ways. Many people, when working with their subconscious mind, will process things in pictures and images. This helps them "experience" the lies and truth in a helpful way. It has been said, "a picture is worth a thousand words" and this can be true in a Renew Ministry session.

For example, people may not just feel an Identity Lie, but have a visual picture of it. People may not just "think" what truth Jesus would give them, but may "see" Him communicating that truth in a certain way. Guarding Parts may not just be thoughts, but present themselves as images. Common images occurring in a Renew Ministry session include walls, black balls, boxes, fire, darkness, and a figure or person.

None of this should be interpreted as receiving visions of direct divine revelation from God. Our minds are simply created to process in pictures and to use our imagination to experience truth in a deeper way.

In fact, the Scriptures encourage us to use our imagination. For example, think about the place of imagination in obeying the following command:

> *Since you have been raised to new life with Christ, set your sights on the realities of heaven, where Christ sits in the place of honor at God's right hand. Think about the things of heaven, not the things of earth.* (Col 3:1-2)

You are required to use your imagination to "*set your sights on the realities of heaven*" and "*Think about the things of heaven.*" We are encouraged here to even imagine Jesus sitting at God's right hand. Therefore, it is biblical to imagine Jesus being anywhere at any time. He can be imagined in your memories because He is never limited by space or time. "*Jesus Christ is the same yesterday, today, and forever*" (Heb 13:8).

God expects us to use our imagination to help us experience truth in powerful ways. Certainly, our sinful nature can be used to imagine sin in destructive ways. Accordingly, Christian counselor H. Norman Wright notes:

> Good mental pictures, by involving that half of our mind which we call imagination, will take our understanding further than rational analysis on its own can ever go. This is evidently one reason why Jesus taught in parables and why all communicators do well to cultivate a style of presentation that is as imaginative as it is analytical.
>
> Imagination can rescue us from daily doldrums or lead us to invent a machine. One is tied to escape, the other to discovery. Imagination can also be used to help heal our painful memories and free you from self-condemnation. . . Imagery can be used to bring about the positive changes we seek in our lives. [13]

Using our imagination is especially important when working with Hurting Parts in our hidden heart. Dr. van der Kolk write:

> The imprints of traumatic experiences are organized not as coherent logical narratives but in fragmented sensory and emotional traces: images, sounds, and physical sensations. Therefore, visualization is important. It has been proven that emotional trauma shuts down areas of the brain that control speech, but stimulate brain areas

responsible for visualization. . . Also, it has been demonstrated that emotional events are experienced with the right (visual) part of the brain, not the left (logical) part. [14]

All of this is why we invite people to use their God-given imagination to mentally process in pictures. For example, we ask Recipients to imagine their Hurting Parts in a room. This has proven to have several benefits. First, it helps the Recipient focus on the part of their mind that needs renewal. Secondly, it helps us simplify complex parts, separating out their various components. Thirdly, we have found that the room imagery can decrease the emotional intensity and expenditure in the session, without diminishing its effectiveness. This helps to avoid unnecessary emotional pain in the session, and allows the Recipient to process for longer.

However, if you are more of a "conceptual" thinker instead of a "visual" one, or are simply uncomfortable with introducing imagery in the session, please just tell your Helper. In such a case you will probably be able to process effectively without it. [15]

A Renew Ministry Helper will never encourage you to imagine or visualize something beyond what is prescribed in the Renew Ministry Process. Encouraging Recipients to place things in "Rooms" has proven to be a safe and helpful step in the Process. However, Helpers are not authorized to encourage whatever imagery they might think will be helpful. They are only to respond to the images your mind might create in answering the prescribed questions of the Renew Ministry Process. [16]

## 9) God is usually <u>not</u> interested in answering "why" questions

Renew Ministry deals with the impact of the most tragic and painful events in your life. It is common to want to know "why" God allowed such things to happen. There are theological answers to that question that are most clearly answered in the book of Job. But those answers rarely help people in the midst of their pain.

What will actually relieve your pain is <u>not</u> having an answer to "why did God allow that to happen." Rather, the source of your pain is an Identity Lie that was imprinted by the experience and made you feel worthless, alone, etc. Revealing and resolving <u>that</u> will relieve your pain and you probably will no longer care about answering the "why" question.

## 10) You are probably more free than you think

Often the significance of the transformation that occurs in a Renew Ministry session will not be recognized immediately. But in the days and weeks ahead, when you experience circumstances that previously triggered the Identity Lie you resolved, you will discover that you are not even tempted to feel the way that you use to. The freedom you accomplished in a Renew Ministry session will become more evident as time goes by.

▶ Complete Project 1 by taking some time to review the "Primary Principles of Renew Ministry" on the next page. Ensure that you understand them.

---

12 Bessel van der Kolk MD, *The Body Keeps the Score* (Penguin, 2014, Kindle ed.), 204, 211, 219).

13 H. Norman Wright, *Making Peace with Your Past* (Revel, 1985), 50.

14 van der Kolk, 43-45.

15 A *Wikipedia* article on "Visual thinking" relates the following:

Visual thinking, also called visual/spatial learning or picture thinking is the phenomenon of thinking through visual processing. Visual thinking has been described as seeing words as a series of pictures. It is common in approximately 60–65% of the general population. . .

"Real picture thinkers", those who use visual thinking almost to the exclusion of other kinds of thinking, make up a smaller percentage of the population. Research by child development theorist Linda Kreger Silverman suggests that less than 30% of the population strongly uses visual/spatial thinking, another 45% uses both visual/spatial thinking and thinking in the form of words, and 25% thinks exclusively in words. (online at https://en.wikipedia.org/wiki/Visual_thinking)

16 If you are looking for a respected, Christian, and professional opinion about the use of imagery in counseling, you can read Dr. H. Norman Wright's chapter on the topic in his book, *Self-talk, Imagery, and Prayer in Counseling* (W Pub Group, 1986), in the highly regarded professional series, *Resources For Christian Counseling*.

Project 1
# Primary Principles of Renew Ministry

1) **The Spirit's Power.** Authentic Christianity is consistently experiencing the unconditional powers of God's Spirit in you which include love, joy, and peace.

2) **Feelings**. Everything you feel is empowered by what you are believing. Feelings are not always a good guide to what is true, but they reveal what you really believe.

3) **The Spirit/truth vs. Sin/lies.** Believing lies empowers your sinful nature producing anger, worry, discouragement, etc. Believing the truth empowers God's Spirit in you, producing His fruits of unconditional love, joy, and peace.

4) **Transformation.** Because you are controlled by what you believe, you can *"be transformed by the renewing of your mind"* (Rom 12:2) and replacing the lies you believe with the truth. This transformation is radical and permanent.

5) **Identity Lies & Hurting Parts.** The Devil's only weapon is a lie. Specifically Identity Lies about God's love for us. The most common is a belief that we are worthless or alone. These Identity Lies are very painful and create Hurting Parts that need the truth of God's love to set them free.

6) **Your Past.** Through painful experiences in your past, the Devil has established *"fortresses"* (2 Cor 10:4) and *"footholds"* (Eph 4:27) of Identity Lies in your subconscious mind that greatly affect your life.

7) **Guarding Parts.** Guarding Parts often obstruct the resolution of Hurting Parts deceived by Identity Lies. These often include feeling afraid or ashamed. And often result in analytical thinking, anger, or the suppression of painful emotions or memories.

8) **God Lies.** God Lies are imprinted in painful circumstances where we are deceived into being disappointed and hurt by God. Because God is the source of the truth we need, these must be resolved for Hurting Parts to be set free.

9) **Hidden Parts of Your Heart.** Mind renewal must include the subconscious mind to be effective. Most Christians do not need more truth, but rather they need the truth they already have in more places of their mind.

10) **Emotions & Logic.** Connecting with negative emotions allows us to access the hidden part of our heart and reveal the lies it believes. Asking "Why" questions and what Jesus would say, engages the logical mind and allows us to transfer the truth there to renew the hidden, hurting, and deceived parts of our mind.

Chapter 4
# The Seven Steps in a Renew Ministry Session

Below are seven Basic Steps in a Renew Ministry session. It will be helpful for you to review them because understanding the process makes Renew Ministry sessions much more effective:

1) CONNECT

2) FEELING

3) EXPERIENCE

4) LIE

5) JESUS

6) TRUTH

7) REVIEW

If interference in these steps is encountered because of a Guarding Part or God Lie (as described later in this chapter), then additional questions are asked to resolve these.

Each Step has a purpose that is accomplished by answering prescribed questions. These purposes, questions, and helpful instructions for the Renew Ministry Recipient are briefly described below for each Step.

## THE CONNECT STEP

| **CONNECT** Connect to Jesus | **Connect Question #1:** "How do you feel about being here today?" *Negative response: Go to Guarding Part Process.* |
| | **Connect Question #2:** "How does Jesus feel about you being here today?" *Negative response: Go to God Lie Process.* |

The purpose of the Connect Step is to connect with Jesus as well as expose God lies and Guarding Lies early on.

## A) Connect with Jesus

It is often helpful for recipients to find some measure of comfort and security in Christ before moving on to focusing on painful emotions. This can be seen as securing your harness before diving in. Also, it is normal to feel nervous and anxious before a session, especially for new people, and this helps calm those anxious parts.

## B) Expose Guarding Parts and God Lies early on

These two questions may also flush out God Lies or Guarding Parts (God Lies and Guarding Parts are discussed on p. 38) early in the process. This often makes for a smoother session with less Guardian Parts and God Lies later on.

## C) Don't be surprised if you spend a lot of time in the Connect Step

This step is intentionally designed to flush out God Lies and guardian parts, so do not be surprised if you spend whole sessions in this step. This is progress! Many individuals have never explored their emotions in this setting before and may have a lot of guarding parts keeping them from diving in. Also, many individuals have never thought about how Jesus feels toward them in a meaningful way, so it is very important for them to work through this before moving on.

## D) It's okay to skip this step

This step may especially be helpful for new people who are not used to diving into their painful emotions. For those that appear more comfortable exploring their negative emotions right away, this step may be skipped. Use your best judgement in this area.

# THE FEELING STEP

| **FEELING**<br>Find a deeper emotion | **Focus Question:** "What negative feeling are you struggling with?"<br><br>**Why Question:** "Why do you feel that way?"<br><br>**How Question:** "How does that make you feel?" *Repeat Why and How Questions until they express a strong and specific emotion.* |
| --- | --- |

The purpose of the FEELING is to focus on one strong negative emotion. Emotions are central to the Renew Ministry process. This is because the target of Renew Ministry is the hidden and hurting parts of your subconscious mind. Because this part of your mind operates on emotion, you need to access, embrace, and analyze feelings to resolve controlling Identity Lies.

This is perhaps the hardest part of Renew Ministry for most people. The feelings produced by lies are painful. Normally we are trying to suppress anger, fear, shame, etc. In a Renew Ministry session we are asking you to let these things "come to the surface" so you can face them, reveal their source, and permanently resolve the lies that are causing them. Some additional guidance for the FEELING Step includes:

## A) No need to accurately label feelings

You do not need to describe your feelings with an accurate label. It is sufficient to just say, "It feels bad." Or "it hurts." Your Helper does not need to know the specific feeling and sometimes you may not be able to specifically label it. Describe it the best you can.

## B) Must experience the feelings

It will not be sufficient to just "talk about" your feelings. What is important is that you are actually FEELING them. Only then can we know that we are ministering to the right place in your heart. If your feelings are somewhat vague and difficult to "connect" to, your Helper may ask you something like, "When is the last time you felt that way?" Discussing recent experiences that were challenging or upsetting can help you experience the feelings you need to resolve.

### C) Come to the session with a negative feeling to work on

It can be helpful to monitor your feelings throughout the week and make at least a mental note of something that "triggered" you to feel negative and sinful emotions. This will be a good place to begin a session.

### D) Try to focus on one feeling

Some struggle to have any feelings at the beginning of a session. But others are struggling with a lot of strong emotions. It will probably not help you to just "vent" about all of your problems and struggles. The sooner you can focus on one feeling/issue and begin resolving it, the better.

## THE EXPERIENCE STEP

| EXPERIENCE Find associated experience or theme | Experience Question #1: "As you focus on that feeling what comes to mind?" |
| --- | --- |

Connecting to a past painful event will help you connect better to a hurting and hidden part of your heart. Our mind has an amazing ability to "associate" current feelings with past events where we experienced the same thing. Doing so is not always necessary but usually helpful. Some additional guidance for the EXPERIENCE Step includes:

### A) Don't "remember" events, but instead follow feelings.

Again, it is important to work with the subconscious mind. Therefore, focusing on following the feeling, will lead you to a hidden and hurting part. If you try to "remember" painful events logically, you will probably not be accessing a hidden and hurting part of your heart.

This is why we do not begin by asking you about your past or have you try to remember painful events. This would tend to simply engage your logical/conscious mind. By starting with feelings, and focusing on and following those feelings, we are working with your subconscious mind.

Dr. Smith shares:

> To demonstrate how association works, think about the word "CLASSROOM." What just happened? A memory probably surfaced. Did you see how quickly that occurred? Notice that you did not have to try or look for a memory about a classroom.
>
> Now think about the words "FIRST KISS." Whoa! Bet you didn't see that one coming. This is how God designed your mind to work. It is natural, automatic, and effortless. The associative process is not a strange and mysterious thing, but rather, the natural outcome of mentally focusing on something.
>
> If the facilitator has explained to the person how God has designed our minds to naturally "associate" to a memory, then the person can *relax* in their emotion and allow their mind to do what it was designed to do.

## B) Specific events or general themes will work

It is common to simply connect to "themes" instead of one specific event. Something like, "My dad was always angry." This is fine. What is again important is that you are experiencing negative emotions and connecting with a hidden and hurting part of your heart.

## C) Don't underestimate the significance of a past experience

Do not dismiss what first comes to mind in answer to Experience Question #1 in the EXPERIENCE Step. Often you will have no idea how it relates to the feeling/issue you are working with in the FEELING Step. Likewise, what comes to mind may seem unimportant. But the first thing that comes to mind has proven to be where people need to go.

Do not worry about not understanding how your current feelings are connected to a past event. Most people will not know this initially. Do not dismiss a memory because you cannot immediately make this connection.

After things are resolved in the session, the significance of the event and the relationship between things will be more clear.

### D) Your perception matters, not reality

Some are concerned that they may not remember something accurately. First of all, no one does. No one perfectly remembers everything or knows everything about a particular event. Especially events that occurred in our childhood.

Thankfully, it does not matter. What matters is how <u>you</u> remember something because that is <u>your</u> reality and what may have imprinted you with a painful lie. If a memory comes to mind and gives you negative feelings, then it is a source of a painful lie you believe. What you must resolve then is <u>your interpretation</u> of what happened, not necessarily what actually happened. [17]

### E) It will not be necessary to share all the details of a past event

In fact, you do not need to share any details. The only purpose of the EXPERIENCE Step is simply to be better connected to a Hurting Part. Then you can answer the questions in the LIE Step about how this part feels and why.

### F) It's OK if these places feel childish

Remember, hidden and hurting parts of your heart are stuck back in time when they were hurt. When you re-experience these places, it may feel a little odd because you may be dealing with a childish part of your mind.

### G) It's OK if you have to visit a specific event several times

Some painful events create several Hurting Parts and Identity Lies. Therefore, it may be necessary to work with a particular event in several sessions. This is normal and does not mean you are not making progress. Each time you resolve an Identity Lie that was created by a painful event you are making progress.

# THE LIE STEP

| | |
|---|---|
| **LIE**<br>Reveal painful bottom lie | **Why Question:** "Why do you feel that way?"<br><br>**How Question:** "How does that make you feel?"<br>*Repeat Why and How Questions until they respond with an emotional Identity Lie. Usually, a version of worthless or alone.* |

This is where the real "battle" is: Searching the hidden parts of your heart to find the deceived and hurting parts. These things are usually not on the "surface" and require some "digging." It is necessary to get to the "bottom" of these hurting parts which will be a painful Identity Lie.

A good analogy is pulling weeds. It is easy to just pull the top off of a weed. But unless you pull up all the roots, the weed will just grow back. So it is with the Lie Fortresses in the hidden and hurting parts of your heart. You must find that painful Identity Lie in the bottom of the dungeon of that fortress in order to set it free. The "truth" will not work until the bottom Identity Lie is revealed. Some additional guidance for the LIE Step includes:

## A) Report any hesitancy or interference to answering a question

This Step is probably working with some very painful places in your heart. It is important to proceed slowly and not force things, resolving Guarding Parts and God Lies along the way.

## B) Don't be frustrated by the repeated questions

This Step can last 20-30 minutes of asking the *Emotion* and *Belief* questions over and over again: "How does that make you feel?" and "Why do you feel that way?"

Why do these questions need to be repeated over and over again? Because we are working with your emotional, irrational subconscious mind. Because it is "subconscious" it is not "aware" of the lies it believes. It must be helped to "discover" what it believes. And this requires a patient and seemingly tedious process of asking and answering these questions repeatedly. Along these lines, Dr. Smith notes:

> There have been some people who have complained that the questions [in the LIE Step] can become redundant and monotonous and even frustrate the person receiving ministry. This is understandable if the person receiving ministry is uninformed as to why these questions are being asked. However, for the person who has been taught well and is oriented to the process, the questions make sense and the person will flow with the process. He hears the "redundancy" as a reminder for him to dig deeper, look in new directions or to clarify. This is why it is so important to train the recipient with the process as well as the principles and concepts.

### C) Don't take shortcuts to the Identity Lie

You will discover that by far the most common Identity Lie that you are looking for is a version of feeling "worthless." Sometimes it will be a version of feeling "alone," "hopeless," or "powerless." But knowing these things and trying to "logically" discern or discover them will not help you. You must let your subconscious/emotional/irrational mind REALIZE these painful Identity Lies. And that simply requires repeatedly answering the *Emotion* and *Belief* questions in the LIE Step with the first thing that comes to mind.

# THE JESUS STEP

| **JESUS**<br>Recognize and resolve Guarding Parts | **Jesus Question #1:** "Let's isolate this part of you that feels _____.  If we could bring Jesus to see you feeling that way, how would He feel towards you?"<br>*If Jesus responds with anything other than compassion: Go to the God Lie Process.*<br><br>**Jesus Question #2:** "How does this part of you feel toward Jesus?"<br>*Negative response: Go to the Guarding Part Process.* |
| --- | --- |

The main purpose of the Jesus Step is to recognize Guarding Parts and God Lies.

## A) Guarding Parts

A Guarding Part is a deceived part of you that acts to protect a Hurting Part. Also referred to as a "Guardian Lie." They are the "defense" and "coping" mechanisms created in painful events to keep you from experiencing the pain fully. Examples include parts that act and feel angry, distracted, confused, or ashamed. These hinder or block the Recipient from progressing to deeper emotions and pain in the Renew Ministry session.

Sometimes you will encounter up to 3-6 Guarding Parts (and/or God Lies) in one session. Do not be overwhelmed or confused by this. Simply, diligently, and patiently recognize them and continue to "divide and conquer" them.

Recognizing and resolving Guarding Parts and God Lies is the most difficult part of Renew Ministry. Almost all recipients will encounter them, especially in the beginning sessions. If they are not recognized and resolved the session will not progress to revealing an Identity Lie and healing a hurting part of your heart. As the recipient, assume that guarding parts will be operating at times and be sure to report any sense of resistance or hesitancy on moving forward to your helper. This will greatly increase the effectiveness of the session.

A skilled Helper can notice a Recipient struggling with a question and go to the JESUS Step to determine if a Guarding Part or God Lie is operating. But it is often helpful if the Recipient is willing to report this lack of focus or peace about answering a question. The questions above help to recognize Guarding Parts and God Lies. There are additional questions the Helper will use to enable the Recipient to resolve them on page 44.

## 1) Don't be frustrated if you encounter a lot of Guarding Parts or God Lies

These can seem to be an unnecessary obstacle that needs to be pushed aside so the session can progress and be helpful. But Guarding Parts and God's Lies are not merely distractions hindering a Renew Ministry session. They are deceived parts of you that probably effect almost every day of your life. Resolving them will not only make Renew Ministry sessions easier and faster, but more importantly it will change your life in a significant and permanent way.

## B) God Lies

A God Lie is a false belief about God that is attached to a Hurting Part. These are sometimes referred to as a "false Jesus." Examples include a belief that God is angry, disappointed with, or condemns a Hurting Part. This often results in the Hurting Part feeling anger, shame, or fear toward God.

Obviously, God Lies will hinder a Hurting Part from receiving the necessary truth of God's love to set it free from the Identity Lie controlling it. Therefore, it is necessary to recognize and resolve any God Lies that a Hurting Part believes. One purpose of the Jesus Step is to detect any God Lies attached to the Hurting Part you are ministering to by asking how Jesus feels toward the part. Any lack of compassion from Jesus always indicates a God Lie.

# THE TRUTH STEP

| **TRUTH**<br>Experience<br>the truth | **Truth Question:** "If Jesus interacted with you, what would happen?"<br>*Negative response: Go to the God Lie Process.*<br><br>**Emotion Question:** "How does that make you feel?"<br>*Negative response: Go to Lie Step.*<br><br>**Test Question #1:** "Are there any other negative feelings in this place?"<br>*If yes, ask: "How would Jesus respond to that?" If still unresolved, go to Lie Step.*<br><br>**Test Question #2:** "Let's return to any past or present experiences. How do those places feel now?" (Recheck each memory visited in order from least to most recent.)<br>*If unresolved emotions, ask: "How would Jesus respond to that?" If still unresolved, go to Lie Step.* |
|---|---|

This is the fun part! The dawn after the darkness. The new victory after feeling the pain of past defeat! Here you will experience Jesus after confronting the painful lies of the Devil. Because we have revealed the "bottom" Identity Lie in the LIE Step, you are now ready to receive and experience in a new way the freeing truth about God's love. Some additional guidance for the TRUTH Step includes:

## A) We are depending on the truth you already know from Scripture, not miraculous revelations from Jesus

In the Truth Question we are attempting to personalize the truth by making Jesus its source. In fact, visual thinkers may experience the mental processing in the TRUTH step in the form of pictures.

But the Truth Question is worded carefully to avoid the impression that we are expecting direct divine revelation. By asking, "How would Jesus interact with this part of you?" we are appealing to the historical Jesus revealed in Scripture, not a new, present, and personal revelation from Jesus. Jesus physically appeared and audibly spoke to the Apostle Paul (cf. Acts 9:4-6; 18:9-10). This is not the kind of experience that occurs in a Renew Ministry session.

Therefore, a Renew Ministry Helper will <u>NEVER</u> ask you a question like, "What is Jesus saying to you?" or "What is Jesus showing you?" Nor will a Renew Ministry Helper claim to have a "prophecy" or "word of knowledge" for you. A miraculous operation of the Holy Spirit or a supernatural divine revelation is not needed to *"be transformed by the renewing of your mind"* (Rom 12:2).

What is practically happening in the TRUTH Step is that the truth you already trust in your logical/conscious mind is simply being transferred to a part of your subconscious/emotional mind. God created our minds to do this and the Renew Ministry process works to facilitate it.

## B) Jesus is not bound by time

Often the painful Identity Lie you are addressing was experienced in a painful event. In the TRUTH step, some people will object that they cannot receive the truth of Jesus in that place because they did not have a personal relationship with Him at the time. But *"Jesus Christ is the same yesterday, today, and forever"* (Heb 13:8). Even if you did not know

Jesus when a painful event occurred, you can apply His truth now to the Identity Lie that was formed from a past event.

## C) Testing freedom

Test Question #1 is designed to test if the Identity Lie has been replaced with the truth. You will know this has happened if the painful feelings have been replaced with peace. Often people will say that place or part feels "better" or "good."

## D) Sadness

When asking the Test Question #1, sadness may be present even though the painful Identity Lie has been replaced with freeing truth. Sadness is often a truth-based emotion and a legitimate feeling about the painful experiences addressed in the session. God is also sad about these things too. Grieving is often very appropriate. If you report a remaining sense of sadness, the Helper will simply ask something like "What would Jesus say about that?" This usually brings significant comfort.

## E) Residual issues

Even when the painful Identity Lie is resolved, some experience remaining questions in that place or from the renewed part. Again, the Helper will simply ask what Jesus would say about these things and they are usually easily resolved.

## F) Experiencing your new freedom

Test Question #2 is designed to give the Recipient an opportunity to experience their new freedom from the Identity Lie. This lie previously caused negative feelings in a present circumstance discussed in the FEELING Step and perhaps in past events encountered in the EXPERIENCE Step. The Helper will use Test Question #2 to help you revisit these places. Usually people will feel very different about these circumstances, giving further evidence that mind renewal has occurred.

# THE REVIEW STEP

| **REVIEW** Process and close the session | **#1:** "What lie did this hurting part believe?" **#2:** "How has this deceived part of you effected your life?" **#3:** "What was the truth that this hurting part realized today? |
|---|---|

The questions in the REVIEW Step help you to briefly meditate on what you discovered in the Renew Ministry session. As a result, Recipients often have a deeper understanding of the renewal that occurred, and realize several additional applications of the truth they have newly experienced.

▶ Complete Project 2 by taking some time to review the "Renew Ministry Steps" on the next page. Do not be overwhelmed by it. You do not have to understand it all, your Helper will. But this helps you be familiar with the Process. If you have any questions about a Step, ask your Renew Ministry Helper.

---

[17] For more on the concerns about ministering to memories see the *Renew Ministry Training Manual*, chapter 9 section D.

Project 2
# The RENEW Ministry Steps: The Basic Process

| | |
|---|---|
| **CONNECT**<br>Connect to Jesus | **Connect Question #1:** "How do you feel about being here today?"<br>*Negative response: Go to Guarding Part Process.*<br><br>**Connect Question #2:** "How does Jesus feel about you being here today?"<br>*Negative response: Go to God Lie Process.* |

| | |
|---|---|
| **FEELING**<br>Find a deeper emotion | **Focus Question:** "What negative feeling are you struggling with?"<br><br>**Why Question:** "Why do you feel that way?"<br><br>**How Question:** "How does that make you feel?"<br>*Repeat Why and How Questions until they express a strong and specific emotion.* |

| | |
|---|---|
| **EXPERIENCE**<br>Find associated experience or theme | **Experience Question #1:** "As you focus on that feeling what comes to mind?" |

| | |
|---|---|
| **LIE**<br>Reveal painful bottom lie | **Why Question:** "Why do you feel that way?"<br><br>**How Question:** "How does that make you feel?"<br>*Repeat Why and How Questions until they respond with an emotional Identity Lie. Usually, a version of worthless or alone.* |

| | |
|---|---|
| **JESUS**<br>Recognize and resolve Guarding Parts | **Jesus Question #1:** "Let's isolate this part of you that feels _____.  If we could bring Jesus to see you feeling that way, how would He feel towards you?"<br>*If Jesus responds with anything other than compassion: Go to the God Lie Process.*<br><br>**Jesus Question #2:** "How does this part of you feel toward Jesus?"<br>*Negative response: Go to the Guarding Part Process.* |

| | |
|---|---|
| **TRUTH**<br>Experience the truth | **Truth Question:** "If Jesus interacted with you, what would happen?"<br>*Negative response: Go to the God Lie Process.*<br><br>**Emotion Question:** "How does that make you feel?"<br>*Negative response: Go to Lie Step.*<br><br>**Test Question #1:** "Are there any other negative feelings in this place?"<br>*If yes, ask: "How would Jesus respond to that?" If still unresolved, go to Lie Step.*<br><br>**Test Question #2:** "Let's return to any past or present experiences. How do those places feel now?" (Recheck each memory visited in order from least to most recent.)<br>*If unresolved emotions, ask: "How would Jesus respond to that?" If still unresolved, go to Lie Step.* |

| | |
|---|---|
| **REVIEW**<br>Process and close the session | **#1:** "What lie did this hurting part believe?"<br><br>**#2:** "How has this deceived part of you effected your life?"<br><br>**#3:** "What was the truth that this hurting part realized today? |

# RENEW Ministry Steps: Resistance Process (Table 1)

| GUARDING PART PROCESS | |
|---|---|
| Before moving on, asking the Why and Truth Questions will resolve more simple and less painful Guarding Parts. | |
| **Isolate the Guarding Part** (Checking first for a God Lie that is attached to the Guarding Part) | **Guarding Part Question:** "Let's isolate this part of you that feels _____. Let's recognize this part has been protecting you, but has been deceived and is keeping Jesus from healing the hurt here. If we brought Jesus to see this part of you, how would He feel towards you?" *Negative response: Go to God Lie Process.* |
| **Resolve the Guarding Part** | **Truth Question:** "If Jesus interacted with this part of you what would happen?" *Negative response: Go to God Lie Process.* <br><br> **Emotion Question:** "How does that make this part feel?" *Negative response: Ask Why and Truth Questions.* <br><br> **Test Question:** "Is this part of you willing to yield to Jesus?" *Negative response: Ask Why and Truth Questions.* |

# RENEW Ministry Steps: Resistance Process (Table 2)

| GOD LIE PROCESS | |
|---|---|
| **Reveal God Lie** | **Expose Question:** "What would this Jesus want to say or do to this Hurting Part of you?" |
| **Isolate False Jesus** | **Isolate:** "Let's take this Jesus who [would feel, do, say the answer to Expose Question]. Isolate him." |
| **Resolve God Lie** | **False Jesus Question:** "If we brought the Jesus of Scripture, who died for you on a cross, to see this False version of Himself, how would he feel?"<br><br>**Truth Question:** "If we let the Jesus of Scripture interact with this False version of Himself, what would happen?"<br><br>*For multiple God Lies: See "Multiple God Lie Process" in the Renew Ministry Training Manual.* |
| **Return to Basic Process** | **True Jesus Question:** "Let's bring the Jesus who loves you back to this Hurting [or Guarding] Part. If this Jesus could see this Part of you, how would He feel?"<br><br>*If you have the true Jesus, continue with Guarding Part or Basic Step you were working with. If another God Lie, see "Multiple God Lie Process" in the Renew Ministry Training Manual.* |

Chapter 5
# Renew Ministry Requirements I: Humility
James 4:6-7, 10

Renew Ministry is about layers. Layers of painful events to be visited. Layers of lies to be resolved. Layers of Guarding Parts and God Lies to be revealed. Layers of hurting parts to be healed. Dealing with all those layers will be one of the most painful experiences in your life.

The renowned Christian author C. S. Lewis gave us a picture of what this painful resolution of layers looks like. In his *Voyage of the Dawn Treader*, he tells us of a young boy named Eustace. The young man is selfish, stubborn, and sinful. As a result, he becomes a big ugly dragon. But the pain of experiencing the consequences of his sinful nature creates a desire within him to change.

But he cannot do this himself. Eventually the great lion Aslan (representing Jesus) appears to him and leads him to a pool of special water to bathe in. But because Eustace has become a big dragon, he is too large  to enter the pool. Aslan tells him to undress. Eustace remembers that he can cast off his skin like a snake. So, he takes off a layer by himself, dropping it to the ground, making him feel better. But as he moves to the pool, he realizes he is still too large and that there is another hard, rough, scaly layer still on him.

Feeling frustrated, in pain, and longing to get into that beautiful bath, Eustace asks himself, "How many skins do I have to take off?" After three layers, he gives up, realizing he cannot do it himself. Aslan then says, "You will have to let me undress you." To which Eustace replies:

> I was afraid of his claws, I can tell you, but I was pretty nearly desperate now. So, I just lay flat down on my back and let him do it. The very first tear he made was so deep that I thought it had gone right into my heart. And when he began pulling the skin off, it hurt worse than anything I've ever felt. . .
>
> Well, he peeled the beastly stuff right off, just as I thought I'd done it myself the other three times, only they hadn't hurt. And there it was lying on the grass: only ever so much thicker, and

darker, and more knobbly looking than the others had been. And there was I, smooth and soft . . .

Then he caught hold of me and threw me into the water. It smarted like anything but only for a moment. After that it became perfectly delicious and as soon as I started swimming and splashing I found that all the pain had gone from my arm. And then I saw why. I'd turned into a boy again. . . After a bit the lion took me out and dressed me with his paws in these new clothes I'm wearing. [18]

Like Eustace, embracing the layers of Guarding Parts and Identity Lies in your life will be painful. Remember, though, this is only because the lies you believe about yourself are so painful. But also, like Eustace, you will discover in Renew Ministry that Jesus Christ and His truth will do a powerful and wonderful work to set you free from controlling lies about who you are. But even Eustace had to choose to put himself in a position for Aslan to effectively help him. The Bible says that position is humility.

**God opposes the proud but gives grace to the humble. So humble yourselves before God. Resist the devil, and he will flee from you. . . Humble yourselves before the Lord, and he will lift you up.** (James 4:6-7, 10)

Stop fighting God and start defeating the Devil.

## A) God opposes the proud

Christian, God your Father loves you deeply. He sent His Son to suffer and pay for all your sins. And when this life is over, He is going to bring you into an eternal and perfect Paradise to live with Him. David described your Father like this:

*The LORD is compassionate and gracious . . . He does not treat us as our sins deserve or repay us according to our iniquities. For as high as the heavens are above the earth, so great is his love for those who fear him; as far as the east is from the west, so far has he removed our transgressions from us. As a father has compassion on his children, so the LORD has compassion on those who fear him; for he knows how we are formed, he remembers that we are dust.* (Ps 103:8-14 NIV)

God your Father deeply and completely loves you. And that is why He will oppose damaging pride in your life. Pride will hurt your life. What would that pride look like? Denying that our spiritual needs are hurting us and hurting others. A refusal to get the help we need. When we have that kind of pride, we will experience God's opposition. A child of God can find themselves actually fighting against God.

God warned of this in the OT: "*O people of Israel, do not fight against the LORD. . . for you will not succeed!*" (2 Chron 13:12). He warned us of this in the NT: "*You stubborn people. . . Must you forever resist the Holy Spirit?*" (Acts 7:51). When a child of God continues to be deceived about their sin, or in denial of it, our Father "*disciplines those he loves*" (Heb 12:6). "*No discipline seems pleasant at the time, but painful. Later on, however, it produces a harvest of righteousness and peace for those who have been trained by it*" (Heb 12:11 NIV). "*Righteousness and peace*" are God's goals for allowing hardship and pain in our life.

As explained in the previous *FRUIT* study:

> He loves you enough to protect you from the dangers of pride and denial to bring painful things into your life to humble you. He so desires that you have an accurate and honest understanding of your true spiritual condition that He will allow your spiritual weaknesses to intensify and become so painful and destructive that you will no longer be able to deny they are there. But again, this is all to help you. "*God opposes the proud*" to teach them to be "*humble*" so He can give them His "*grace*," power, and blessing. [19]

Dr. van der Kolk describes the potential results of our pride and refusal to admit our need for help:

> As long as you keep secrets and suppress the truth, you are fundamentally at war with yourself. Hiding your true feelings takes an enormous amount of energy. It saps your motivation to pursue worthwhile goals, and it leaves you feeling numb and shut down.
>
> Meanwhile, stress hormones keep flooding your body, leading to headaches, muscle aches, problems with your bowels or sexual functions—and irrational behaviors. Behaviors that may embarrass you and hurt the people around you. Only after you identify the source of these responses can you start to be free from them. . .

Silence about trauma also leads to death—the death of the soul. Silence reinforces the godforsaken isolation of trauma. Being able to say aloud to another human being, "I was raped" or "I was battered by my husband" or "My parents called it discipline, but it was abuse" or "I'm not making it since I got back from Iraq," is a sign that healing can begin.

We may think we can control our grief, our terror, or our shame by remaining silent, but naming them offers the possibility of a different kind of control. If you've been hurt, you need to acknowledge and name what happened to you. I know that from personal experience: As long as I had no place where I could let myself know what it was like when my father locked me in the cellar of our house for various offenses, I was chronically preoccupied with being exiled and abandoned. Only when I could talk about how that little boy felt, only when I could forgive him for having been as scared and submissive as he was, did I start to enjoy the pleasure of my own company.

Feeling listened to and understood changes our physiology; being able to articulate a complex feeling, and having our feelings recognized, lights up our limbic brain and creates an "aha moment. [20]

Because our Father loved His people, He appealed to His prideful children who were afraid to change:

*It was I, the LORD your God, who rescued you from the land of Egypt. Open your mouth wide, and I will fill it with good things. But no, my people wouldn't listen. Israel did not want me around. So I let them follow their own stubborn desires, living according to their own ideas. Oh, that my people would listen to me! Oh, that Israel would follow me, walking in my paths! How quickly I would then subdue their enemies!* (Ps 81:10-14)

God reminded His people that He rescued them. And He has done the same for you: "*He has rescued us from the kingdom of darkness and transferred us into the Kingdom of his dear Son, who purchased our freedom and forgave our sins*" (Col 1:13-14). He promises that if we will turn to Him to receive from Him, He "*will fill* [us] *with good things.*" But sometimes we continue to ignore Him and He lets us "*follow* [our] *own stubborn desires"* that continue to hurt our life. As a loving Father He pleads with us, *"listen to me."* And He promises if we will *"follow"* Him, He will *"quickly subdue* [our] *enemies"* and help us to be victorious over them.

You have a powerful and cruel enemy who is always working around you and in you to destroy your life" (1 Pet 5:8). And you need God's help *"to destroy the works of the devil"* (1 John 3:8) in your life. Which is why the Bible says: *"God opposes the proud but gives grace to the humble. So humble yourselves before God. Resist the devil, and he will flee from you. . . Humble yourselves before the Lord, and he will lift you up"* (James 4:6-7, 10).

Do you see the connection between being humble toward God and defeating Satan? Humbling yourself before God is resisting the Devil. Being humble toward God makes Satan *"flee from you."* Being humble is the first step to being free from the lies Satan uses to control and hurt your life. Therefore, being humble is the first step to experiencing God setting you free and lifting you up out of your painful and dysfunctional life.

And again, this humility is demonstrated in our willingness to admit our need. David did this when he prayed to God: *"I am poor and needy, and my heart is wounded within me"* (Ps 109:22). Can you admit the same? Stop fighting God and start defeating the Devil.

## B) Resist the devil

Earlier in this booklet, we described how Satan gains control of our lives through Lie Fortresses (cf. 2 Cor 10:4). And how he protects those Lie Fortresses with Guarding Parts:

> Guarding Parts are places in your mind that have been working to help you cope with the emotional pain inside of you. They have helped you suppress, deny, or be distracted from these painful emotions like feeling worthless or alone. . .

> Therefore, Guarding Parts have performed a God-ordained and helpful function to keep us "going" in spite of all the emotional and spiritual wounds we carry. But the Devil has perverted them to serve his purposes. Guarding Parts are deceived. They have no relationship with God. In reality, they are powers of your sinful nature and will power. They cause powerful feelings of anger, fear,

shame, and doubt. The Devil uses our Guarding Parts as the protective "wall" around the Lie Fortresses within us. These walls of anger, fear, shame, and doubt keep us from recognizing, revealing, and resolving the IDENTITY LIES in our Lie Fortresses.

Guarding Parts keep you from being connected to, and controlled by, God and His Spirit in you. Jesus Christ wants to replace or renew these Guarding Parts with His love and truth. [21]

The Devil has probably constructed such "walls" to protect his Lie Fortresses in your mind. These walls are usually made of FEAR, PRIDE, and SHAME.

FEAR is the visible outer surface of these walls. We say this because FEAR about discussing your spiritual condition or past painful experiences is the most apparent indication that Satan has sinful fortresses controlling your life. Deep down, it is a FEAR of being rejected if people knew more about you. You must trust God to be open with someone about your spiritual struggles. If you do not, Satan will continue to control you from his fortress in your mind and your life will not change.

The substance of these walls that Satan puts around his fortresses is PRIDE. PRIDE is always protecting some kind of PAIN. It causes you to put a "mask" on so that you seem more significant and secure than you really feel. But ironically, PRIDE is usually the confident looking "shell" that is protecting and hiding our FEAR. If you have things in your life that you feel embarrassed about, PRIDE will cause you to protect yourself. And in doing so, you protect Satan's fortresses in your life. This is one reason why the Bible warns: *"Pride leads to destruction; a proud attitude brings ruin"* (Prov 16:18 NCV).

PRIDE causes the FEAR that keeps you from being open about how the Devil has hurt you. It comes from the belief that your value and acceptance depend on your performance or how people view you. This is why some of the most confident looking people actually have a great deal of FEAR in them. And this is one of the best ways to detect PRIDE in your life. Do you FEAR people? Do you FEAR people knowing about your weaknesses and struggles? If so, it is because your PRIDE causes you to believe your true value and acceptance depends on what people think of you.

For all of these reasons, the Bible says three times: "*God opposes the proud but gives grace to the humble*" (Prov 3:34; 1 Pet 5:5; Jms 4:6). If you have destructive and protecting PRIDE in your life, God loves you enough to humble you so He can give you his grace, power, and blessing.

Finally, deep inside and underneath our PRIDE and FEAR is SHAME. Shame is caused by an underlying and deep doubt about the love and grace of Christ. It is probably the most powerful weapon the Devil uses to keep people from recognizing and destroying his Lie Fortresses in their minds. SHAME serves Satan. It keeps the Devil's work inside of you in the dark, and he has power in the darkness.

The feelings and attitudes of FEAR, PRIDE, and SHAME lead to the action of DENIAL. This is the practical effect of the "walls" of painful lies Satan has created in your mind to protect his sinful "*stronghold*" (2 Cor 10:4). You are in DENIAL if you automatically think painful events in your past are better off forgotten. Simply ignoring a wound will not keep it from festering. You are in DENIAL if you ignore or underestimate the degree of your sin or how much it is hurting you and others.

Denial of our sin and spiritual struggles can lead to even deeper self-deception. First, we start making excuses for our sin. Then we even begin to falsely blame others for our sin. We are ultimately responsible for our sinful responses to people sinning against us. "No one makes us mad." [22] And all of those excuses and blaming will only leave us trapped in our deception, pain, and pride.

This is why the Bible warns us: "*God opposes the proud but gives grace to the humble. So humble yourselves before God. Resist the devil, and he will flee from you. . . Humble yourselves before the Lord, and he will lift you up*" (James 4:6-7, 10). Stop fighting God and start defeating the Devil.

How do you heal your SHAME? It must be gently but fully brought into the loving light of Jesus Christ. And how will you do that? How do you overcome SHAME? By believing the truth that those dark and dirty parts of you ARE NOT YOU. Often, they represent things that were done to you by truly dark and dirty people. But you Christian are not dark and dirty. God says, "*You were once darkness, but now you are light in the Lord*" (Eph 5:8 NIV).

Our SHAME sometimes comes from the lie that we are somehow uniquely sinful or damaged or challenged. Not true. God's word reminds us that the struggles and sins and pain we have experienced are unfortunately common in this world (cf. 1 Cor 10:13; 1 Pet 5:9). This is not to invalidate your pain in any way. But the truth is that your Renew Ministry Helper has probably ministered to people who had sins, struggles, and experiences that were very much like yours. They probably will not be surprised by your story. There is no reason to believe they will reject you because of how you have been hurt and are hurting.

Renew Ministry is not intended to push you where you do not want to go. It is designed to gently but effectively deal with your FEAR and SHAME and other obstacles that keep you from experiencing Jesus' promise that *"the truth will set you free"* (John 8:32).

How do you know you are being humble? The Bible says:

> All of you, dress yourselves in humility <u>as you relate to one another</u>, for "God opposes the proud but gives grace to the humble." So <u>humble yourselves under the mighty power of God</u>. (1 Pet 5:5-6)

Do you see the connection between being humble with people and being humble with God? What does this humility toward people look like in Renew Ministry? Just being willing to be honest about your feelings. Being willing to talk about things that have hurt you in your past. Being willing to do the hard work to be free that we discuss in the next chapter.

All of this is why the Bible says: *"God opposes the proud but gives grace to the humble. So humble yourselves before God. Resist the devil, and he will flee from you. . . . Humble yourselves before the Lord, and he will lift you up"* (James 4:6-7, 10). Stop fighting God and start defeating the Devil.

▶ If being open about your sin and struggles is challenging for you, it might help to read the chapter on this elsewhere in the *Christian Essentials*, study #2 *FOUNDATIONS*, "The Power of Openness." In that study you are encouraged to have God Times following the P.O.W.E.R. plan which includes being "Open" with God. Practicing this will help you have the necessary openness to process effectively in Renew Ministry.

---

[18] See C. S. Lewis, *The Voyage of the Dawn Treader*, (Collier, 1970), 90–91.

[19] Excerpt from *the FRUIT Study*, chapter 2 section B.

[20] Bessel van der Kolk, *The Body Keeps the Score* (Penguin, Kindle edition, 2014), 233.

[21] Excerpt from the FREEDOM Study, chapter 11 section A.

[22] For more on our ultimate responsibility for sinful responses to sinful people see *the FRUIT Study*, chapter 4 section B, "No one and nothing MAKES you mad, afraid, or discouraged"

Chapter 6
# Renew Ministry Requirement II: Hard Work
James 1:4

Humans are constantly seeking products and programs that will radically change the quality of their life, with as little cost, time, and effort as possible. But anyone who has lived for very long will tell you that the saying is true: "You get what you pay for." The search for something that is powerful, but easy or cheap will usually lead to disappointment and a waste of your time and money.

The same is true of spiritual growth. Christians are looking for something that will radically change them and help them experience the power of the Holy Spirit's love, joy, and peace. But they often do not want to invest the necessary time and effort to accomplish this. The Apostle Paul wanted to correct this false and worldly thinking about spiritual growth when he told Timothy, *"Train yourself to be godly"* (1 Tim 4:7).

The word *"train"* translates the original Greek word *gymnaze*. Obviously, we get our words gymnastics and gymnasium from this word. It was used in Paul's time to refer to the very difficult and even painful training that ancient Olympic athletes would commit to in order to increase their physical strength or skill. Like the example of the Christian gymnast Gabby Douglas above, there was perhaps no greater example of training in Paul's day than the Olympic athletes. Which is why he used their example elsewhere in Scripture when he wrote: *"Everyone who competes in the games goes into strict training"* (1 Cor 9:25 NIV).

Likewise, when God commands us to *"train yourself to be godly"* (1 Tim 4:7) He wants us to work hard at our spiritual growth. Bigger and stronger muscles and more conditioned bodies do not just happen without our effort. Physical growth requires work. And so does spiritual growth.

Notice that it is your responsibility to *"train yourself to be godly"* (1 Tim 4:7). God is commanding and expecting you to do this because you have the ability to do it. This brings up a foundational truth of the Christian life: GOD IS NOT GOING TO DO FOR YOU WHAT HE HAS ALREADY ENABLED YOU TO DO.

So, what is God's part in your spiritual growth? *"God is working in you, giving you the <u>desire</u> and the <u>power</u> to do what pleases him"* (Phil 2:13). This *"desire"* and *"power"* to be godly comes from His Spirit living in you. If God's Spirit lives in you, you will never lose your *"desire . . . to do what pleases"* God. But the *"power"* to be godly does not happen automatically. You have a necessary part to play to *"train yourself to be godly"* (1 Tim 4:7) and experience the Spirit's power.

And that necessary part for you to play in your spiritual growth has been the topic in the *FREEDOM* study and is also described in the following verse:

**Let perseverance finish its work so that you may be mature and complete, not lacking anything**. (James 1:4 NIV)

If there is no pain, there is usually no gain in spiritual growth.

## A) The worthwhile gain of Renew Ministry

This verse is about cost and reward. Before talking about the cost, notice the reward! To *"be mature and complete, not lacking anything"*! As discussed elsewhere in the *Christian Essentials*, we do not believe the Bible teaches that we can become a constantly perfect person in this life. We will sin until the day we die, or Jesus comes back. But we must not ignore the full meaning of what a person indwelled with God's Spirit can become. [23]

Twice in this verse, the Greek word *teleios* is used. This is a very rich word that usually refers to something reaching its end goal, or being *"mature and complete"* as it is used in James 1:4. NT scholar William Barclay comments that the idea here is that a person becomes "fit for the task they were sent into the world to do." [24]

In the context, the *"mature and complete"* person is contrasted with those whose *"loyalty is divided between God and the world, and they are unstable in everything they do"* (James 1:8). To be *"mature and complete"* here means to have a united heart, a healed and renewed heart, that loves God. And that is worth a lot.

You only have one life to live. In order to make the most of it, you must be free of the hurting and deceived parts of your hidden heart. You must *"be transformed by the renewing of your mind"* (Rom 12:2 NIV). And when you are, the benefits and blessings of that will be too many to number. But let's just try a "top ten" of the wonderful results of being a *"mature and complete"* Christian:

#1: You will be closer to God, having a more intimate relationship you're your Father like Jesus had.

#2: You will be as close as you can be to actually obeying the Greatest Commandment to *"Love the Lord your God with all your heart and with all your soul and with all your mind and with all your strength."* (Mark 12:30)

#3: You will *"produce much fruit"* and become *"true disciples"* of Jesus, living a life that *"brings great glory to* [your] *Father."* (John 15:8)

#4: You will fulfill one of your ultimate purposes in life which is the *"goal to please him"* (2 Cor 5:9 NIV), giving your Father joy, instead of grieving His Spirit in you (cf. Eph 4:30).

#5: Because you will be consistently obeying Jesus' *"commandments"* *"you will be filled with* [His] *joy. Yes, your joy will overflow!"* (John 15:10-11)

#6: Because Jesus Christ is consistently living through you, you will make the most of this life and have a great and eternal impact on the people in your life.

#7: Because you will be consistently controlled by the Holy Spirit, you will consistently experience His love, joy, and peace (Gal 5:22) regardless of your circumstances.

#8: Because you will be consistently controlled by the Holy Spirit, the commands of Christ and the high demands of the Christian life will feel like an *"easy"* yoke and *"light"* burden (Matt 11:30).

#9: You will be free from the pain, destruction, and shame that comes from sinful anger, bitterness, envy, lust, depression, fear, and addictions.

#10: You will make the most of your eternity because you stored up more treasure in Heaven, and built your life on precious things, instead of worthless and wasted things that will just burn up. (cf. Matt 6:19-21; 1 Cor 3:12-15)

What would you be willing to do in order to accomplish all of that with your short life on this Earth? What would it look like if, rather than putting so much effort into controlling your behavior, you put the same amount of effort into transforming your life? What if you put more effort into GROWING Christianity, instead of COPING Christianity? COPING is hard work too. Exhausting. But it provides no lasting progress. GROWING by being *"transformed by the renewing of your mind"* is hard work too. But at least it results in radical and permanent change.

But that requires you to *"Let perseverance finish its work"* (James 1:4). Specifically, the perseverance and hard work required to *"be transformed by the renewing of your mind"* (Rom 12:2) by healing the hurting and hidden parts of your heart. The Bible teaches that, if there is no pain, there is usually no gain in spiritual growth. But the gain is awesome, and God will make sure it is well worth the pain.

## B) The necessary pain of Renew Ministry

It is obvious that God made our bodies so that it requires some work and even pain to grow and strengthen our muscles. The same is true of growing spiritually. It requires work, perseverance, and even some pain. The Apostle Paul described the nature of spiritual growth when he wrote: *"Endurance develops strength of character"* (Rom 5:4). Perseverance through painful difficulties and challenges is necessary to grow our faith and spiritual maturity.

But why is this? Because faith in God grows through experience. You can read about God's power and love in the Bible. But you especially grow in your relationship with God when you personally experience Him. How did the Israelites learn to depend on God? He led them into a desert and revealed Himself to them. Later Moses explained:

> *He humbled you, causing you to hunger and then feeding you with manna . . . to teach you that man does not live on bread alone but on every word that comes from the mouth of the Lord.* (Deut 8:3)

Experiencing the love and power of God in a painful place is the most powerful way that we grow in our relationship with God.

And this is both the hardest and the very best thing about Renew Ministry. It will probably require you to recognize and minister to some painful parts and places of your life. Things you have been pushing down inside of you and trying to forget and ignore. But if you are honest, you will realize that ignoring or running away from your painful parts and places does not work. They keep chasing you. Pastor Scazzaro writes:

> Turning toward our pain is counterintuitive. But in fact, the heart of Christianity is that the way to life is through death, the pathway to resurrection is through crucifixion.

> Gerald Sittser, in his book *A Grace Disguised*, reflects on the loss of his mother, wife, and young daughter from a horrible car accident. He chose not to run from his loss but to walk directly into the darkness, letting the experience of that overwhelming tragedy transform his life. He learned that the quickest way to reach the sun and the light of day is not to run west chasing after it, but to head east into the darkness until you finally reach the sunrise. [25]

In Renew Ministry, we gently help you to stop running and turn around and face your "demons" with Jesus. Perhaps you have tried to resolve these painful parts and places in your life before and only experienced pain and defeat. *"But thanks be to God, who always leads us in triumph in Christ"* (2 Cor 2:14). We follow God in Renew Ministry sessions and when we do, He *"always leads us to triumph in Christ"* over those scary, overwhelming, painful, and sinful parts and places in our life.

And this brings us to the very best thing about persevering through Renew Ministry: A closer relationship with God. All of the many people who have gone through this process will tell you this is what they appreciate the most. The love of God is more real to them. God is more real to them. And this happened because they EXPERIENCED the love and light of God in the darkest, most deceived, and most painful places in their heart and mind.

You can gain a knowledge of God's love from reading the Bible. But it is experiencing His love that permanently transfers that truth from your mind to your "heart." It is experiencing the truth that builds your faith and sets you free, not just knowledge. And EXPERIENCING GOD is about the best two-word description of what Renew Ministry is. But this will only happen if you persevere.

All of this explains why even God designed mind renewal to require time, work, and even pain. It is a journey, and perhaps a difficult and long one. Why? BECAUSE JESUS WANTS YOU TO EXPERIENCE HIM

ALONG THE WAY. He wants you to gain <u>more</u> than just freedom from painful and controlling lies. He wants a closer relationship with you. And that usually happens in no other way than going through difficult things with Him.[26] Accordingly, one respected and experienced Christian counselor has written:

> One of the chief obstacles to [spiritual] healing is our obsession with the immediate. The "itch for the instantaneous" pervades much of our Christian thinking. We tend to think that unless [spiritual growth] is immediate, it is not of God. We have become impatient and frustrated with things that take time. The truth is that God Himself is going to slow down our pace, for He has no shortcuts to spiritual growth and maturity. [27]

This is because Jesus Christ wants to go on a challenging but victorious journey <u>with you</u>, not just wait at the end when you are done. Those who persevere in Renew Ministry discover that THE JOY IS IN THE JOURNEY, just as much as in the "finish line."

Still, if there is no pain, there is usually no gain in spiritual growth. Which is why the Bible encourages us to, *"Let perseverance finish its work so that you may be mature and complete, not lacking anything"* (James 1:4).

## C) The necessary perseverance for Renew Ministry

There are several aspects of renewing the hidden and hurting parts of your heart that will require perseverance. First, the individual sessions themselves typically require 1.5 to 2 hours. And a great part of that time is spent on you focusing on painful feelings and events that you have suppressed for most of your life. The things you have <u>never</u> wanted to talk about, need to be talked about. The feelings you have <u>never</u> wanted to feel again, need to be experienced. There is simply no other way to heal those hidden and hurting parts of your heart that are hurting your life.

Which is why you will <u>never</u> be looking forward to a Renew Ministry session. <u>Every time</u> several parts of you will tempt you with excuses of why you should not go to your appointment. Let us repeat. You will probably <u>never</u> feel like going to a Renew Ministry appointment. Which is why it is important to remember, if there is no pain, there is usually no gain in spiritual growth. *"Let perseverance finish its work so that you may be mature and complete, not lacking anything"* (James 1:4).

For some, their overall emotional pain from bitterness, anxiety, depression, and shame will consistently decrease with each Renew Ministry session. But for others, their pain will at times increase. Things need to be stirred up that you have wanted to be left alone. Those things may plague you to a greater degree as you work to get them permanently resolved.

But that extra pain is simply Satan's strategy to tempt you to stop messing with him and his territory in your heart. You must trust God with the pain, and trust Him to remove it when you demolish the demonic Lie Fortresses that are causing the pain.

Perseverance will also be needed because of the number of sessions you will need to *"be mature and complete."* There are a few people who may only need a few sessions to be free from their Lie Fortresses. But we would estimate that at least 75% of people will require 1-3 years of weekly sessions to renew all the places in their subconscious mind that have been imprinted with Identity Lies from their past painful experiences.

The bad news is that most of us are more spiritually wounded, broken, hurting, and deceived than we ever imagined. And this will become more apparent to you as you progress through Renew Ministry. Virtually everyone is surprised by how spiritually weak and wounded they really are, and how many sessions it will require to heal those parts, and become *"mature and complete."* Becoming like Jesus is the most important work of your whole life! Do not think that renewing and rescuing the hidden and hurting parts of your heart is going to be accomplished in a couple 30-minute sessions.

The good news is that there is a finite (limited) number of hurting, deceived, and especially controlling parts in your hidden heart. For example, there is a finite number of people you need to forgive. When you do, you will be radically and permanently free from the controlling anger and bitterness caused by whatever that person did to you. When such hurts are resolved, people will be living that level of spiritual health we described as FREER! Christianity in the previous *FRUIT* study. A life where you are consistently controlled by the love, joy, and peace of God's Spirit as God intended you to be.

The really bad news is that most Christians have stubborn and demonic *"strongholds"* (2 Cor 10:4) of Identity Lies hidden in their heart that keep them from becoming who God intended them to be. The really good news is that, *"The reason the Son of God appeared was to destroy the devil's work"* (1 John 3:8 NIV), including the work Satan has done in your life.

The really bad news is that most Christians have experienced painful and traumatic events that mentally imprinted them, emotionally wounded them, and broke a piece of their heart. The really good news is that, *"He heals the brokenhearted and binds up their wounds"* (Ps 147:3 NIV).

The really bad news is that most Christians have parts deep in their heart that are locked up in the dark dungeons of Lie Fortresses, controlled by the Devil, and all too often controlling them. The really good news is that Jesus came to teach us the truth about God's love, and He promised, *"If you hold to my teaching, you are really my disciples. Then you will know the truth, and the truth will set you free."* (John 8:31-32 NIV).

The really bad news is that you have *"your great enemy, the devil. He prowls around like a roaring lion, looking for someone to devour"* (1 Pet 5:8). And he has perhaps devoured and now controls parts of your heart and life. So you must, *"Stand firm against him, and be strong in your faith"* like all the rest of *"your family of believers all over the world"* who are *"going through the same kind of suffering you are"* (vs. 9) because of the Devil's work in their life.

The good news is that IF you will learn to *"stand firm against him, and be strong in your faith"* (v. 9), then *"after you have suffered a little while, he [God] will restore, support, and strengthen you, and he will place you on a firm foundation"* (v. 10).

The really good news is that God's word is full of powerful, wonderful, and life changing promises! You can *"be transformed"* (Rom 12:2), be *"mature and complete, not lacking anything"* (James 1:4), and *"be made complete with all the fullness of life and power that comes from God"* (Eph 3:19).

The challenging news is that most of these promises are conditional. YOU have to be *"renewing your mind"* (Rom 12:2), *"Let perseverance finish its work"* (James 1:4), and seek to *"grasp how wide and long and high and deep is the love of Christ"* (Eph 3:18).

Before God's people crossed the Jordan River to enter the Promised Land, God gave Joshua another one of those awesome but conditional promises: *"I will give you every place you set your foot"* (Josh 1:3 NIV). God wanted His people to conquer all their enemies in the Promised Land and to possess and enjoy everything He had for them there. BUT THEY HAD TO FIGHT FOR IT.

Experiencing and possessing all the blessings of the Promised Land required God's people to trust Him. That was proven by the previous generation, who, *"because of their unbelief they were not able to enter his rest.* (Heb 3:19). Which generation of God's people do you want your life to look like? Moses' generation who wasted forty years of their life wandering in the desert because they would not trust God enough to go with Him and fight to defeat their enemies? Or Joshua's generation that trusted God, fought their enemies, and accomplished God's will for their life?

We have been honest with you. Renew Ministry may be the hardest thing you have ever voluntarily experienced. Other painful experiences have been "forced" on you by people or circumstances out of your control. But experiencing the very temporary but necessary pain to rescue the hidden, hard, and hurting parts of your heart is something you have to choose. As one Pastor testifies:

> My focus was upward and outward — growing our church, reaching people for Christ, raising up leaders, buying a building. But an authentic relationship with Christ also takes us into the depths — the shadows, the strongholds, and the darkness deep within our own souls that must be purged. Surrendering to this inward and downward journey is difficult and painful. [28]

Yes, Renew Ministry takes you to those dark and scary places in your heart. But never forget, the Devil's darkness can never overcome Christ's light (cf. John 1:5). Your darkness is not hidden or scary to Jesus. David said:

> *I could ask the darkness to hide me and the light around me to become night—but even in darkness I cannot hide from you. To you the night shines as bright as day. Darkness and light are the same to you.* (Ps 139:11-12)

But you must be willing to go into the darkness with Him. And that will be temporarily painful. But if there is no pain, there is usually no gain in spiritual growth. *"Let perseverance finish its work so that you may be mature and complete, not lacking anything"* (James 1:4).

---

[23] For more on "perfectionism" and the question of how godly we can become, see *Christian Essentials* study #3 *FAITH*.

[24] *William Barclay's Study Bible*, available online at www.studylight.org.

[25] Peter Scazzero, *Emotionally Healthy Spirituality* (Zondervan, 2006, Kindle ed.), 140-1.

[26] For more on how the difficult "deserts" of life formed the character of several people in the Bible, see Pastor Kurt's book, *Visionary Faith*.

[27] David Seamands, *Healing Memories* (Victor, 1985), 181.

[28] Scazzero, page unknown.

Chapter 7

# Renew Ministry Requirement III: A Heart for God

John 14:15

Kathy has experienced years of Renew Ministry and it has significantly changed her life. She would testify that it has all been very worthwhile. But she was honest when she wrote in response to the question: "What is challenging about Renew Ministry?":

> Everything. Everything. I NEVER want to do Renew Ministry. I ALWAYS want to just avoid whatever is bothering me. I've felt like I can't do Renew Ministry like everyone else can do it, that I'm the defective one. I've been mad at [my Helper] and looked for excuses why this whole thing is crap and I should never go back.

So why did she? Ultimately because she loved God. This is the example that Jesus gave us.

The greatest challenge imaginable was facing Jesus Christ. As He knelt in that garden, He began to feel the weight of the sin that was waiting for Him on the cross. He was anticipating what it would feel like to be PUNISHED for ALL of our SINS and experience the full WRATH of Almighty God. Perhaps even more painful, was the thought of being separated from His Father for the first time in eternity. Because of all this, we are told, *"being in anguish, he prayed more earnestly, and his sweat was like drops of blood falling to the ground"* (Luke 22:44 NIV).

Three times in that garden, our Savior, *"bowed with his face to the ground, praying, 'My Father! If it is possible, let this cup of suffering be taken away from me. Yet I want your will to be done, not mine.'"* (Matt 26:39). In Renew Ministry, you will be constantly confronted with a similar challenge and choice. Again, renewing the hidden and hurting parts of your heart is painful and requires a great deal of time, energy, and sacrifice. And like Jesus, you will want to find another way. An easier and shorter way. Or just to ignore those hurting and controlling parts of your heart altogether.

So why do this? At the resurrection you will be raised a perfect person with no emotional pain, anger, lust, fear, discouragement, or sin at all.

*"We know that when Christ appears, we shall be like him"* (1 John 3:2 NIV). *"God . . . predestined* [us] *to be conformed to the image of his Son"* (Rom 8:29 NIV). You are *"predestined"* to be completely *"transformed"* without doing the hard work of *"renewing your mind"* (Rom 12:2 NIV). So why not wait until that Day when all of this renewal is completely and automatically done for you?

In the previous chapter we offered at least ten reasons, ranging from being closer to God to glorifying God. But there is another reason. It is the ultimate reason. And probably the only reason that will be powerful enough to enable you to do what it takes to *"be transformed by the renewing of your mind"* in Renew Ministry. That reason is this: YOUR LOVE FOR GOD.

Remember, Romans 12:2 is a command. Renew Ministry is not just a nice church program that will help you, and is available if you want to do it. Renew Ministry is a practical and effective way to OBEY THE COMMAND to *"be transformed by the renewing of your mind"* (Rom 12:2). If you want to obey God, then you have no choice but to find the most effective way to do that. Renew Ministry is one of those.

Throughout this study you have read and heard marvelous testimonies about the permanent and radical transformation that people have experienced through Renew Ministry. You've heard about its blessings. But when *"the renewing of your mind"* becomes perhaps the hardest and most painful thing you have ever chosen to do, why will you continue to do it? We are given the answer when Jesus said to us:

**"If you love me, obey my commandments."** (John 14:15)

Only your love for God will be enough motivation to keep you pursuing being transformed by the renewing of the hard and hurting parts of your heart.

## A) The ultimate motivation for Renew Ministry

Often John 14:15 is read as a request from Jesus to prove our love for Him. If we truly love Him, then we will obey Him. This is true. Obeying Him is the proof that we love Him. But there is also a promise here. Jesus said, *"If you love me,"* you will *"obey my commandments"* (John 14:15). Nothing will be able to stop our obedience to Jesus, if we love Jesus. If we love Jesus, obeying Him will always and automatically happen. Love for Jesus is the ultimate reason and power that enables us to obey Jesus.

It turns out that obeying the Greatest Commandment is the ultimate motivation for obeying all the commandments. When you *"love the LORD your God with all your heart, all your soul, all your mind, and all your strength"* (Mark 12:30), you will obey even the hardest commands with joy!

Love for God is why Jesus went to the cross. Nothing else would have been enough, even for Him. In the face of a very painful choice, it was the Son's love for His Father that gave Him the power to sincerely say, *"I want your will to be done, not mine."* (Matt 26:39).

God the Father wanted His Son to love Him by suffering to pay the penalty for your sin. What are you willing to suffer in order to love God by overcoming the power of your sin? The Bible challenges us: *"In your struggle against sin, you have not yet resisted to the point of shedding your blood"* (Heb 12:4 NIV). Jesus was willing to shed His blood to love His Father. We ask you again, what are you willing to do *"in your struggle against sin"*?

Love for God is why Jesus obeyed the most difficult and painful command His Father ever gave Him. The same will be true for you. In Renew Ministry you will discover that Romans 12:2 may be the hardest command in Scripture to actually obey (we will explain that more below). In Renew Ministry you will experience just how hard it is to obey the command to *"be transformed by the renewing of"* the hidden, hurting, hard, and controlling parts of *"your mind"* (Rom 12:2 NIV). And when you realize how hard this will be, only your love for God will be enough motivation to keep you pursuing being transformed by the renewing of the hard and hurting parts of your heart. Which is why Jesus said to his disciples: *"If you love me, obey my commandments"* (John 14:15). [29]

## B) Renew Ministry must be motivated by love, not pain

Understandably, most people begin their journey of mind renewal because they want to get rid of their pain. Their anger, fears, lust, and depression are stealing their happiness and hurting those around them. Their emotional and relational pain is what initially motivates them to get help. And this is O.K. This is even part of God's design. But a mere motivation to reduce your pain will usually not be enough to finish your journey to spiritual freedom.

This is how many approach going to the dentist. We have a toothache. We put up with it for a while because going to the dentist to fix a toothache requires time, money, and is unpleasant. But when the pain of the toothache becomes great enough, we overcome our reluctance and do what it takes to get the tooth healed.

Again, unfortunately, this is how many Christians approach the need to focus a period of time on permanently removing sinful strongholds in their life. They do not pursue this until those strongholds have caused a great deal of pain in their life and the lives of others. There is a better way. It is to pursue GROWING Christianity because you love God. [30]

Ultimately, the desire to heal your pain is rather self-centered. Therefore, when you perceive that the work, time, and even pain of mind renewal is greater than the benefits, you will stop. You will be contented with simply COPING better, instead of being spiritually FREER!, simply because you have experienced a significant decrease in emotional and relational pain.

What will motivate you to continue mind renewal in order to reach the true spiritual freedom and fruitfulness that God wants? YOUR LOVE FOR HIM. Your desire to become more obedient, pleasing, and glorifying to Him. Your desire to love Him with _more_ of your heart, _more_ of your mind, and _more_ of your life. That will be the only sufficient motivation to get you through your journey to the place of spiritual freedom and fruitfulness that your Father has waiting for you.

We encourage you now to make a decision that you are ultimately pursuing transformation and godliness to please and glorify God, instead of just pleasing yourself. Tell God now what Jesus told Him in the garden: "*I want your will to be done, not mine*" (Matt 26:39).

As we said, you will probably experience God in ways you never have before through the Renew Ministry process. But it requires that you love God enough to recognize and resolve whatever parts in your heart that do not yet believe and obey your Lord.

In the previous chapter we listed at least ten amazing results of becoming a "*mature and complete*" Christian. These are wonderful promises for those who "*Let perseverance finish its work so that you may be mature and complete*" (James 1:4). Elsewhere Paul recognizes that such promises are powerful motivations for holiness, but he reminds us of the ultimate motivation when he writes:

> *Therefore, since we have these promises, dear friends, let us purify ourselves from everything that contaminates body and spirit, perfecting holiness <u>out of reverence for God</u>.* (2 Cor 7:1 NIV)

Simply put, God DESERVES for us to do everything in our power to become holier and please and glorify Him with our lives. Can you say in your heart what the popular worship song says?:

> I would run for a thousand years
> If I knew every step would be getting me closer.
> And I'd swim to the ocean floor
> For my Lord is the treasure, my Lord is the treasure. [31]

Only your love for God will be enough motivation to keep you pursuing being transformed by the renewing of the hard and hurting parts of your heart. Which is why Jesus said to his disciples: *"If you love me, obey my commandments"* (John 14:15).

## C) What is the most important commandment to actually obey?
Romans 12:2

We would argue that Romans 12:2 is the most important commandment to obey. Your obedience to all other commands depends on obeying this one. Only to the extent that you are *"transformed"* can you love God and love others. Only to the extent that you are *"renewing your mind"* will you be controlled by the power of the Holy Spirit. And only by being controlled by the Holy Spirit can you obey any of God's commands in a God pleasing way. And obeying Romans 12:2 to *"be transformed by the renewing of your mind"* (NIV) is at the bottom, and the ultimate source, of all these things.

Therefore, we see this necessary "upward spiral" of synergy between renewing our mind and loving God. Which comes first? Renewing our mind. Our initial conversion to Christ demonstrated that. We had no real love for God <u>before</u> we were *"transformed by the renewing of your mind"* with the truth of God's love in the Gospel. And now we must apply all the love for God we have obtained through mind renewal, in order to be motivated to pursue more mind renewal, so we will love God even more.

The Bible reveals a prescribed pattern for spiritual growth and life transformation:

1) Because you love God, make it your goal to obey Him and "*Imitate God in everything you do*" (Eph 5:1). Do not set your sights lower than that, because becoming like Him is His expectation for your life.

2) Let the current level of love you have for God motivate you to pursue obeying Romans 12:2.

3) Be transformed by renewing the logical and subconscious parts of your mind so you will trust the truth of God's love in more places of your heart and life.

4) Then you will be more consistently controlled by God the Spirit who lives inside of you, and will effortlessly and automatically experience His power to obey God so that His commandments are that "*easy*" and "*light*" yoke that Jesus promised.

Obeying Romans 12:2 is the starting point for all of the above. Yes, in Renew Ministry you will learn that renewing those hard and hurting parts of your heart may be the hardest commandment to obey. But the transformation you experience by doing so, will also teach you that Romans 12:2 is among the most important commands to obey. Because when you do, the power of the Holy Spirit will be greater in your life, enabling you to obey all the rest of God's commands automatically and effortlessly. [32]

You will learn in Renew Ministry that only your love for God will be enough motivation to keep you pursuing being transformed by the renewing of the hard and hurting parts of your heart. Which is why "*Jesus said to his disciples: 'If you love me, you will do as I command'*" (John 14:15)

---

[29] See *Christian Essentials* study #2 *FOUNDATIONS* for several more biblical motivations to obey God and do the hard work of being transformed by the renewing of your mind.

[30] Excerpt from *the FRUIT Study*, chapter 32 section B.

[31] "Treasure" by the Desperation Band, copyright, Integrity Music.

[32] Excerpt from *FREEDOM* Study chapter 1 section B.

Made in the USA
Monee, IL
14 July 2024

61793046R00042